The Cranium Cage

OTHER BOOKS BY J.A. HANDVILLE

Internalize

Drowning in the Ink of Oblivion

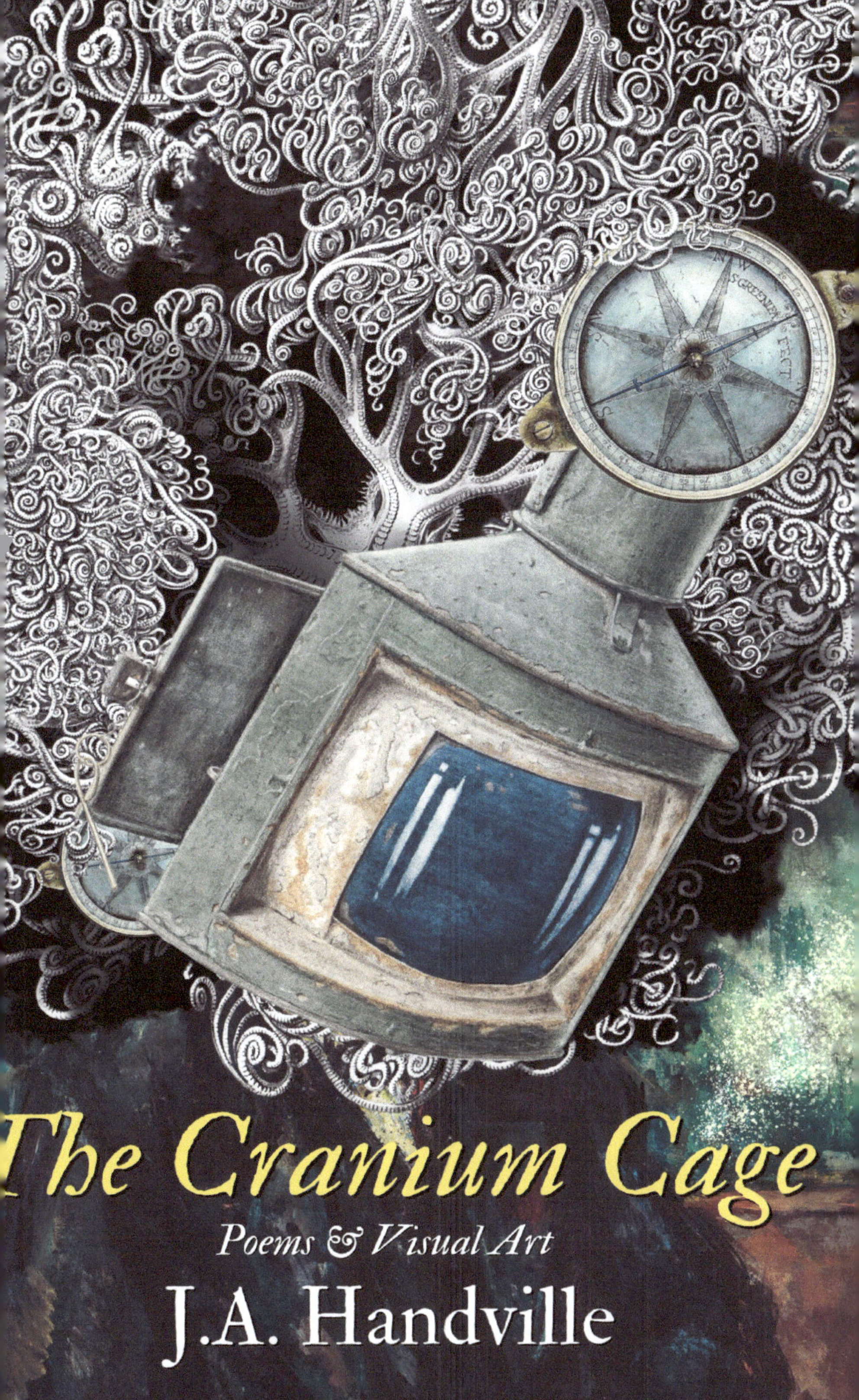
The Cranium Cage
Poems & Visual Art
J.A. Handville

THE CRANIUM CAGE

First edition softcover published in 2025.
Printed in the United States of America.

Book Design & Layout: J.A. Handville
Copyediting: Valerie Valentine
Collage & Cover Artwork: J.A. Handville
Cover Image: *The Cranium Cage*

You can find J.A. Handville on Instagram: @handvilles_studio

ISBN: 979-8-9927480-0-0

This book is dedicated with love to my mother, Danie Maynes, and my grandmother, Sharon Handville – the strongest people I know.

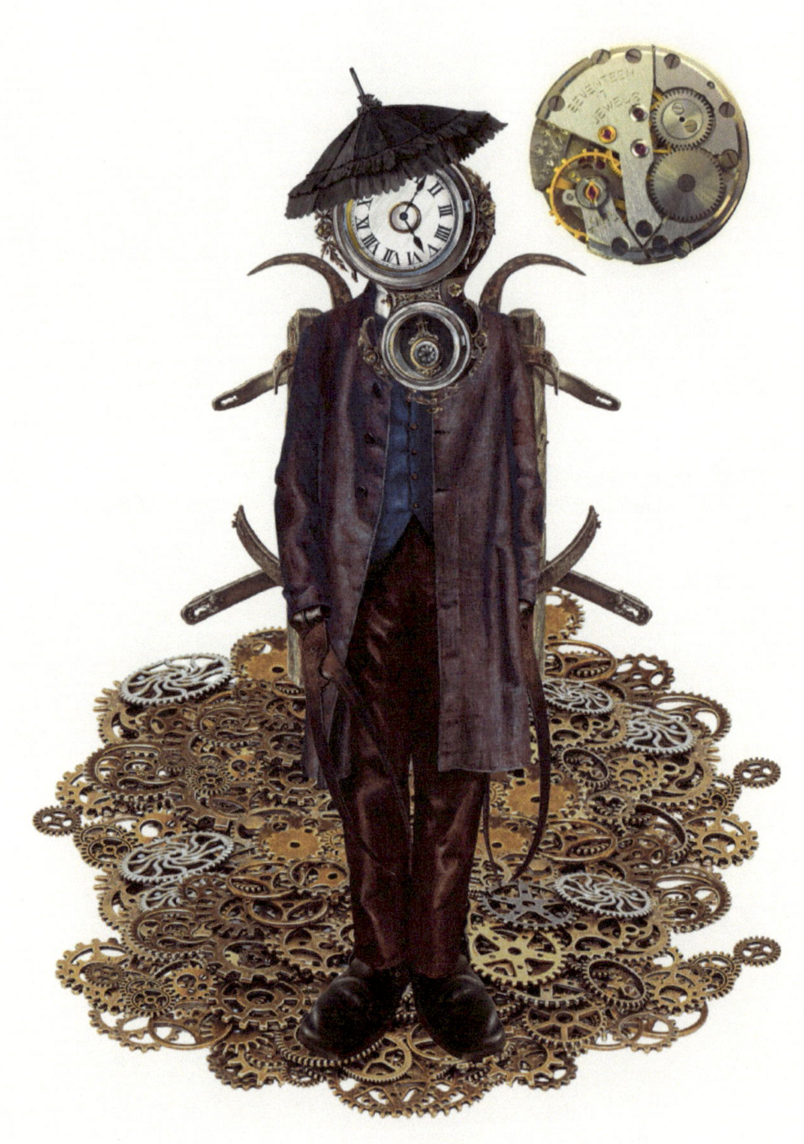

The Ticker, 2024

POETRY

Part One

Part Two

Visual Art

Part One

Part Two

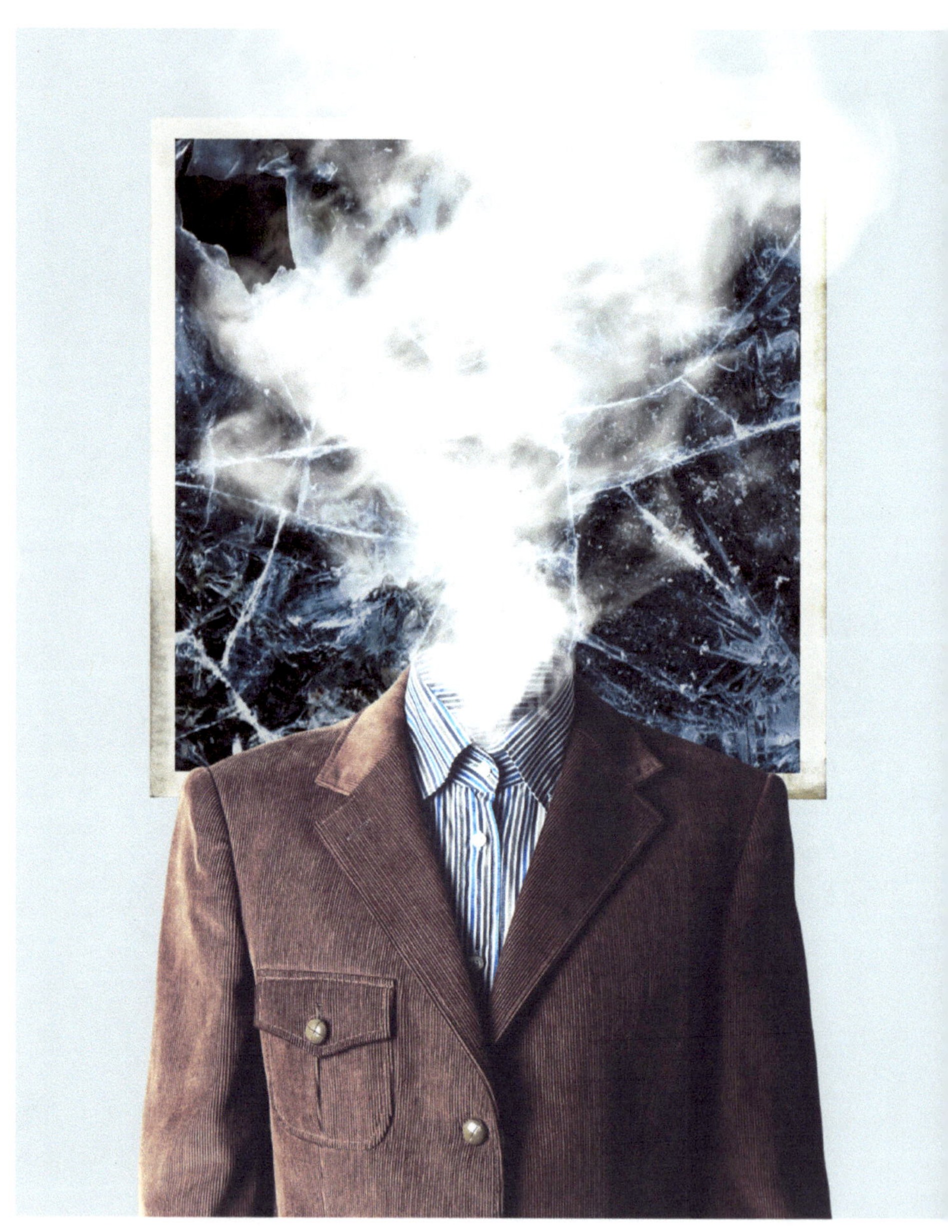

Vanish, 2023

Dear Reader,

Many of the following poems were written between 2018 and early 2021, a period of great inner turmoil, self-sabotage, and stagnation for me. After a public breakdown at work in October of 2019, I began therapy sessions where I was diagnosed with clinical depression. About three months into my sessions, I quit going under the false-but-ever-powerful thoughts that "I do not have it as bad as others," that I should just "get over it" and that I didn't "deserve" treatment. I spiraled thereafter, drinking copious amounts of alcohol and self-sabotaging both friendships and romantic interests in the process. This further fueled my isolation, feelings of alienation, and contemplations of suicide.

I've since grown to understand that navigating my inner turmoil will always be a fight, one that requires my attendance in therapy sessions. I believe, for the first time in a long time, that it's a fight worth pounding my metaphorical knuckles against.

This collection of work presented to you has been a six-year pursuit. I've revised poems beyond what I thought I could produce, incorporated collage artwork to accompany the written material, and painstakingly reworked entire sections of the book from scratch, adding new poems in the process. Admittedly, perhaps my greatest obstacle was overcoming the resistance posed by one nagging question: How could a book rooted in so much darkness be of any worth to others? Since confronting that doubt and uncertainty, I understand that I wish this book to serve a dual purpose.

The first purpose is to serve as a relatable journey for those going through similar experiences, those who may need reassurance that they are not alone in their struggle. I believe we all need to be reminded of that, whether you suffer from mental illness or not. Our thoughts hold the capacity to make us feel so alone at times, and it's important not to allow that feeling to fester.

The second is to serve others beyond just those reading my words, to try to make an impact upon individuals who could truly benefit from having mental health education and services readily available to them.

I've decided to donate a portion of all profits generated from the sale of this book to Mental Health America, a nonprofit dedicated to promoting mental health and providing education and services to those living with mental illness. I hope through our combined efforts, we can make a difference to those who need these resources and services.

Thank you so much for supporting my work and this new, ongoing effort to better the lives of others through it. Take care, stay safe, and try to drown your world in light.

Sincerely,
J.A. Handville

Please be advised: The poetic narrative that serves to detail this period of darkness contains content referring to suicidal contemplation, as well as other potentially disturbing imagery that could provoke intrusive thoughts for those with a personal history with this experience.

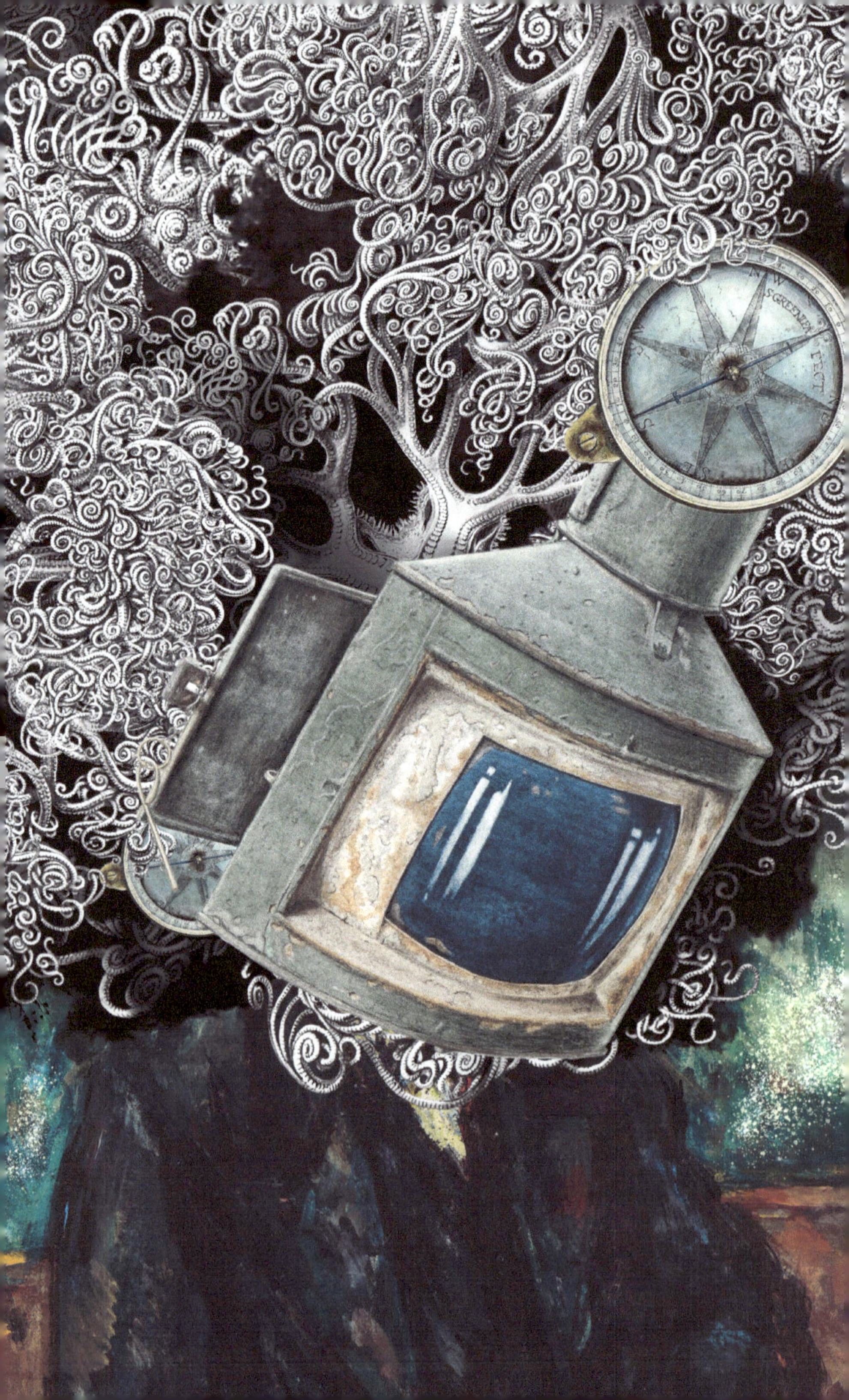

The Cranium Cage

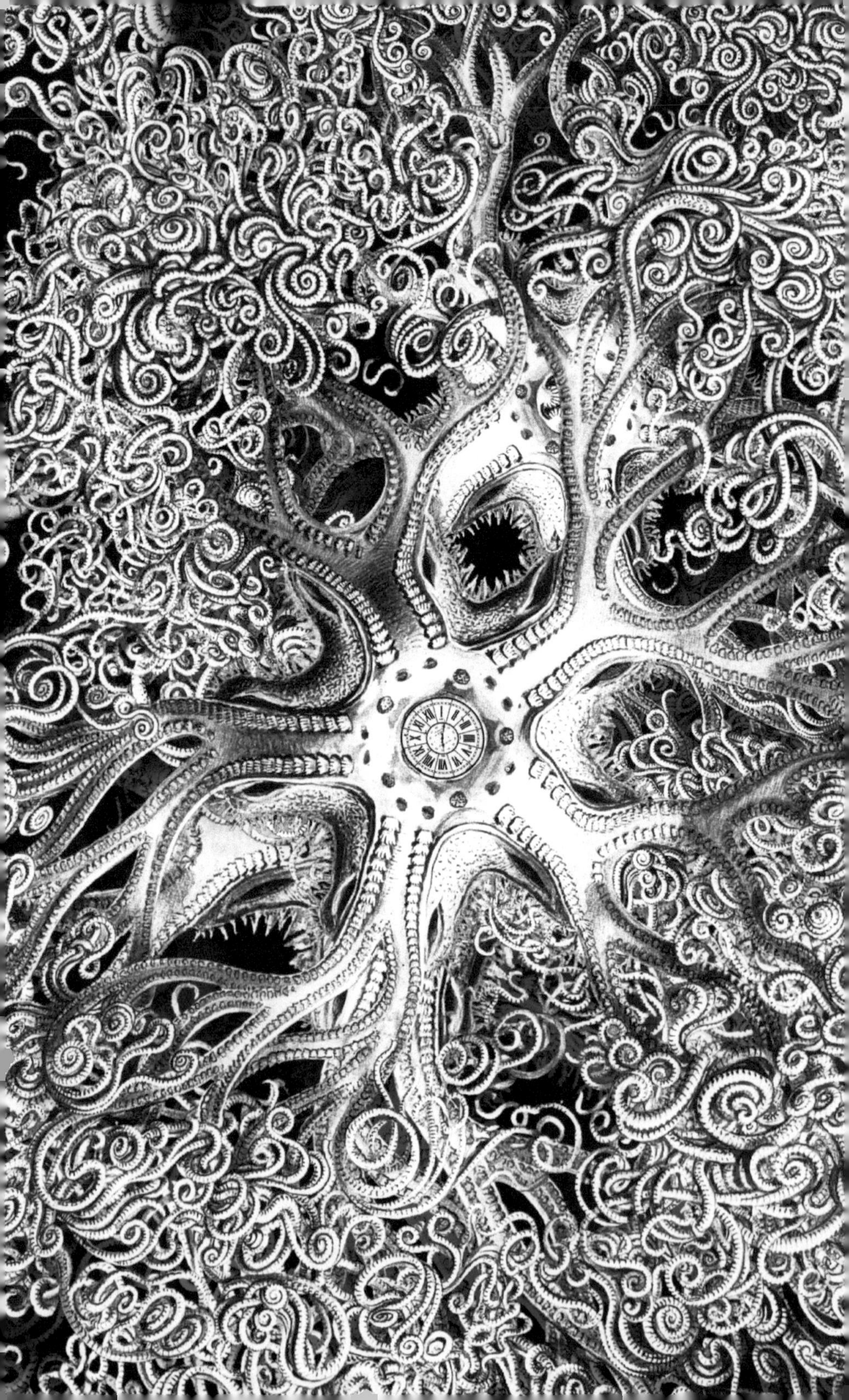

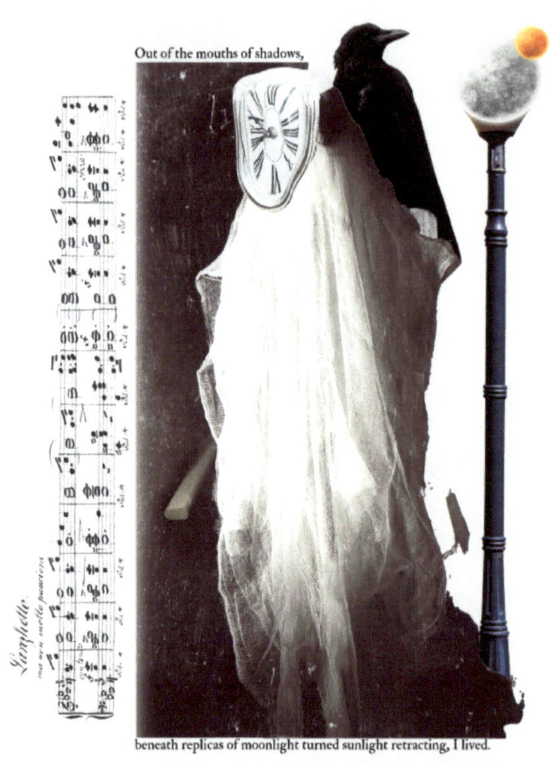

From the Mouths of Shadows, 2022[1]

Echo

It was the year that erupted
out of the mouths of shadows
& the blue lights of televisions.

I lived burned into linen sheets
as a phantom feeding on thread
& twilight, lived
in ghost stories told by the dead
center of a mirror's obedience, lived
in whistling windows watching crows
darken trees, while tumble-dry blankets
of static smothered me
to sleep with bone-thin dreams.

Bedbound, waist thinning
beneath replicas of moonlight
turned sunlight retracting, I lived
tethered by a year that unearthed years.
Sprouted its longevity like time-weathered
roots turned veins turned
tentacles, as they wrapped around
brittle bones & languished limbs,
as my echo-chamber mind screamed
in restless unison
against the claustrophobic constriction.

It was the year that swallowed all others.

Where the future felt like a coin toss
plunged
into the fathomless black ink
of a wishing well.

A Malady's Metamorphosis

My mouth nurtures white moths with wings burnt off

Burnt off & scattered across splinters of spectral sunlight

Spectral sunlight of heatless white: the birth of winter tantrums

Winter tantrums striking wind chimes, shoveling silence

Shoveling silence past a sink bed of drowned porcelain

Drowned porcelain & shipwrecked crumbs: the evidence

The evidence of consumption, left untouched, near the remains

The remains of each meal: an autopsy, after rupturing awake

Rupturing awake in my rogue stomach, I detect nothing's wrong

"Nothing's wrong, nothing's wrong, nothing's wrong," says my mouth

My mouth nurtures white moths with wings burnt off.

Bird of Ill Omen

as a broad flight of quietness
cut my sentences adeptly
without inviting a reason,

in cold air that felt hospitable only
for invisible warnings,
a living death soared en route.

helpless to the weight
of its predatory scale,
a grotesque & vicious raptor,

damned wings spread to sweep
black my own sight
of the sun,

it taunted its talons
before tearing
my identity clean,

my self/me crawling away by belly:
my feigned appearance of escape.
is this surviving?

fearing the wind-rush
of another arrival
to its gluttonous mouth of torment,

where malevolently,
relentlessly,
this living death feeds off me.

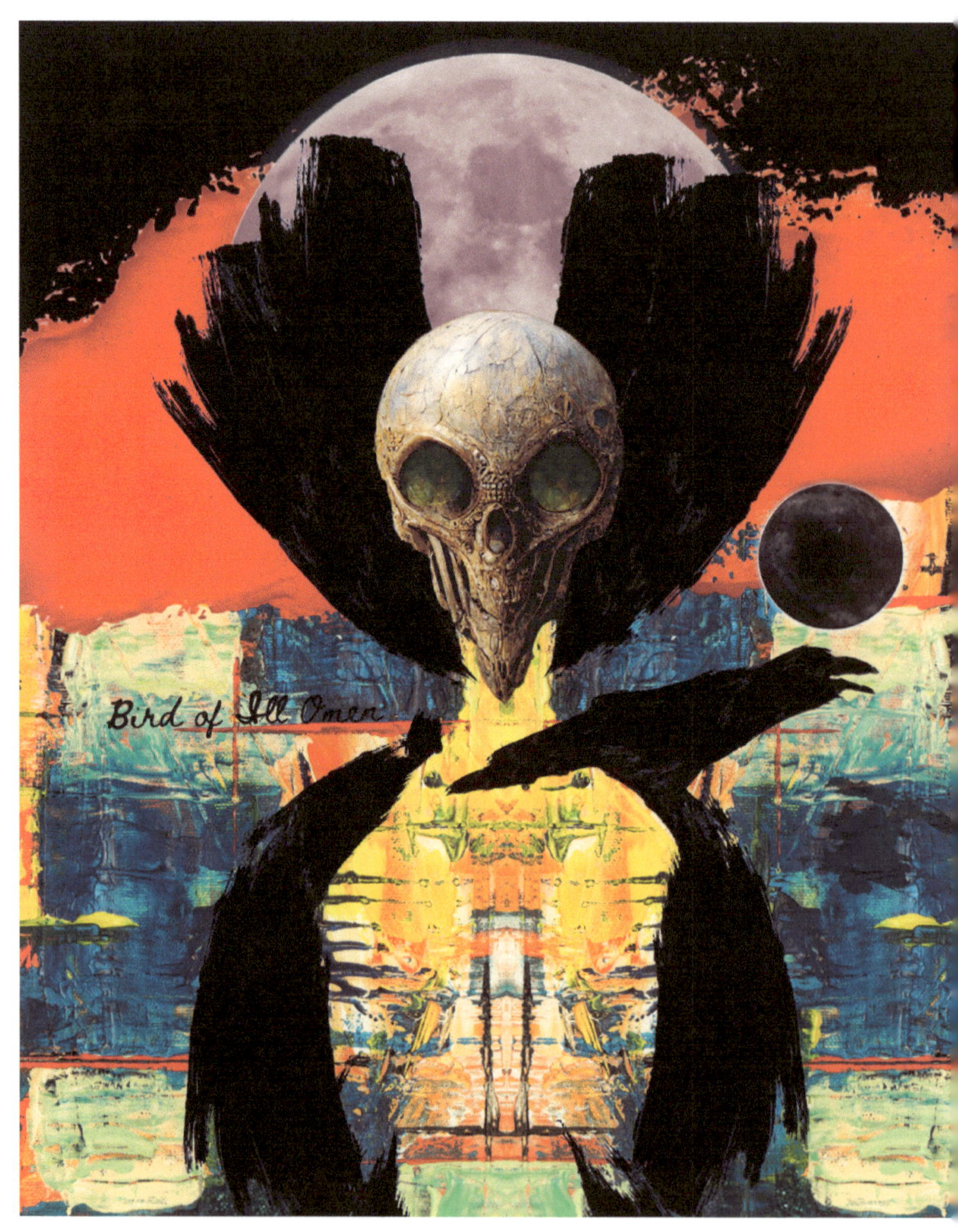

Bird of Ill Omen, 2024

never delivering me
the mercy
of a proper killing.

when will the air of my dreams
taste marvelously
of its smoked flight perfected

by the engulfment
of my projected,
scorching enlightenment.

Crusade

There are no sunsets bleeding blends
of scorching fire that could strip the flesh
from the horrors I've imagined, imagining

suffering outside a mahogany casket
for a co-worker, a friend, a family
member, carved in history unwritten.

Imagined darkness is deemed
mindful preparation.

To feign tranquility then is a crusade against
this great threat I am facing—
fighting claymore to claw, chain mail to bone.

My last act of survival against a tornado
of torment threatening to swallow me
with a smile.

I'm aware this anxiety is a grindstone sharpening
both ends with no regard for the middle.
I'm aware that each ghost of memory leaves me

haunting the present moment. I'm aware
of the ephemeral's sting, of how its loneliness
nurtures me like a newborn cradled beneath
a mother's veiled wing. I'm aware.

& strapped to the torture rack of life's fragility,
rope burns craving confessions carved by a guilty
conscience mentality, I search for some semblance
of frayed peace as my shadow burns heavy against me.

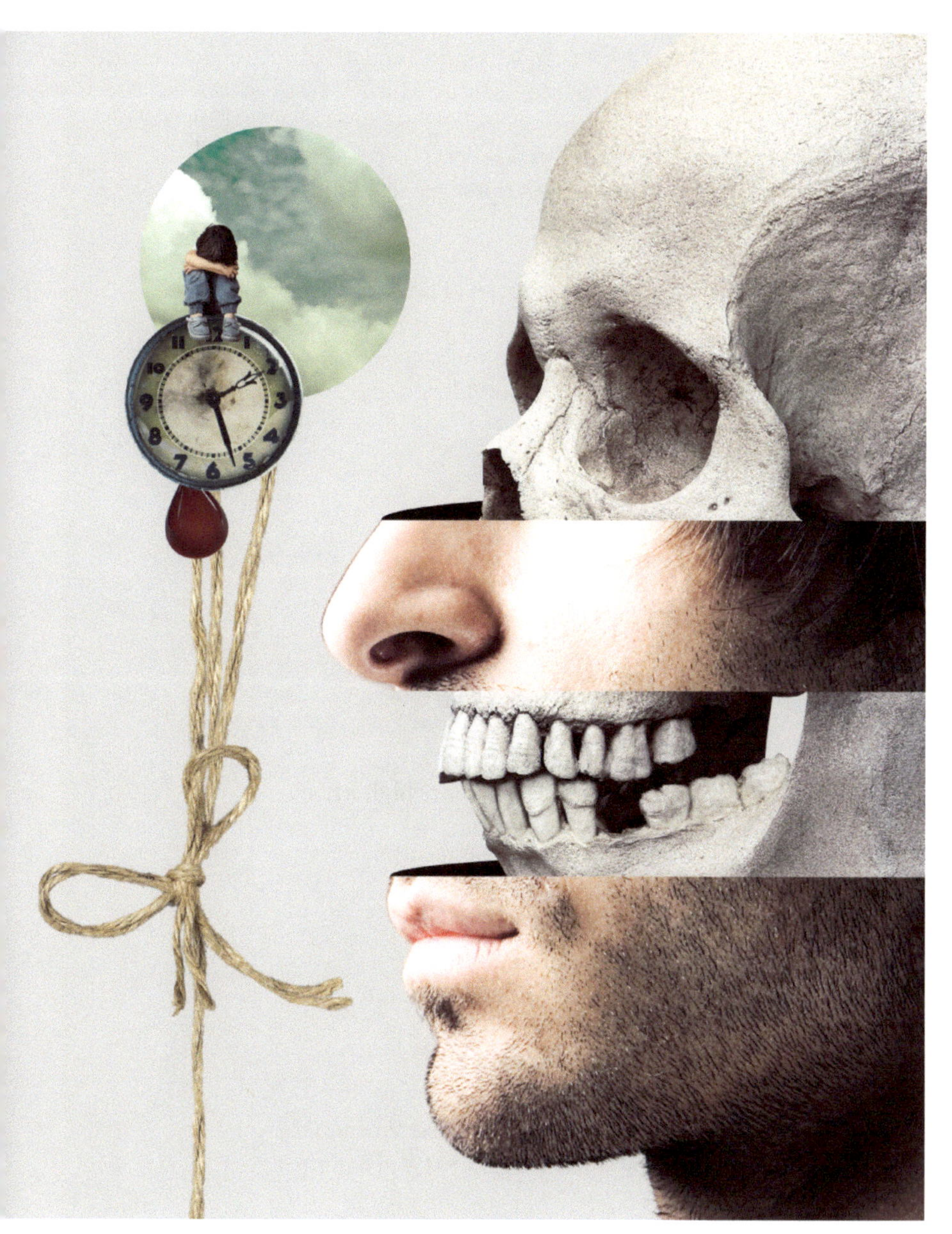

Mortality, 2022

Savior Complex

I have placed myself in this position,
carefully. Treading as if I'm tiptoeing on glass,
more worried about leaving
bloodied footprints behind
than the deep gashes on the soles of my feet.

There are no words, no incantations,
no prayers baptized in a different language,
that I can recite to conjure out
the demon of depression.

& even if there were,
I am a hack exorcist.

But still I am summoned to do so,
exorcise
by the panicked pleading of my ring tone.

I answer
& greet a voice I have not heard since high school.

His tonality is not drenched in desperation
nor loosely sewn with sadness
as he confesses his affliction,
only the suffocating monotone of indifference—
& that's what scares me the most.

I can sense the distance between us.

A distance beyond geographical measurement,
but as small as the last drawn-out letter of a whisper.

A distance,

a distance,

a distance ...

Fractured questions escape my lips,
r e a c h
out to him
but separate within the silence.

Thou art the Creator of all things,
visible & invisible ...

Words become just as lost as I am
within the dead air
that serves as the only connection
between us.

Thou art the Creator of all things,
visible & invisible ...

He tells me he tried to kill himself
last Wednesday.

From the snares of the devil,
deliver us ...[2]

There are no words, no incantations,
no prayers—
yet I'm praying,
praying,
praying in that barren desert of faith,
cracking & crumbling,
knees parallel to the sands
all for a god

who isn't

here ...

Savior Complex, 2022

What is this escalating desperation?

An attempt to save him
or an attempt to save myself?

An act of selflessness
or a rationalized savior complex?

& I hear myself say:
"What difference does that make
if the results
are the same?"

Preachers of Impermanence

It's three a.m. when silence births a swarm
of houseflies buzzing death predictions
like sermons against the drywall. I listen

to those windowsill sounds retreat, drifting
from their altar of indifference before
everything's sacrificed to the almighty

lamp click of *my* reclusive dominion. Yet
here are the dipterans: boisterous, unafraid
to shed life through senseless repetition,

a sure flight of self-certainty, one-way tickets
finished clinging to the questions etched
in the whitewashed flesh of god-fed men,

men repainting themselves pure,
drenched thick with sin but saved
with a daily touch of divinity. Mine lies

in the reclamation of fading memory.
I think of a hue that hushes harbingers
& all other colors plead for forgiveness.

I think of parting dissonance, like the Red Sea,
but sharpen my canine teeth to feast
on the dipterans' own indecision. "Don't you know me?"

I sneer in disgust at the preaching flies
admiring their vanity in crimson reflections.
I catch & crush each blasphemous pulse
& dwell on the decay of my mortal moments.

Suffering

ferments like the gray sludge & stench
of wet papier-mâché, shapes inconsistently
my emotional fluidity, molds me
into invisibility, into my crushed windpipe
in the midst of choking
on nothing—
or is it the first bite of burden born
by rotten fruit in Eden?
my knowledge pale-fleshed
from the hinged act
of desperately chewing
whatever suffering I cannot scour
with goodness,
I will burn into my conscience
with reckless abandon.

What the Beast Desires

a terminal constellation / a polka dot brain / some MRI scans /
no survivability / a car-crash coma / an unconscious sanctuary /
a graveless release / a corpse still breathing / a Van Gogh death /
one gutshot's certainty / a crimson belly painting a commissioned
masterpiece / Hemingway's guilty gun / & one anxious round /
a cleaning kit / an accident / a suicide later found / a host /
some prey / a new mind to lay waste / an old hungry hell lapping
flesh with flame / a life cut short / beneath the taunting of a blade /
or an oven door disguised as an exit sign / singing carbon monoxide
lullabies / perhaps the same that soothed Sylvia to sleep ... / a feast
to ensure hope's deboned & devoured / as a starving servant /
disappears

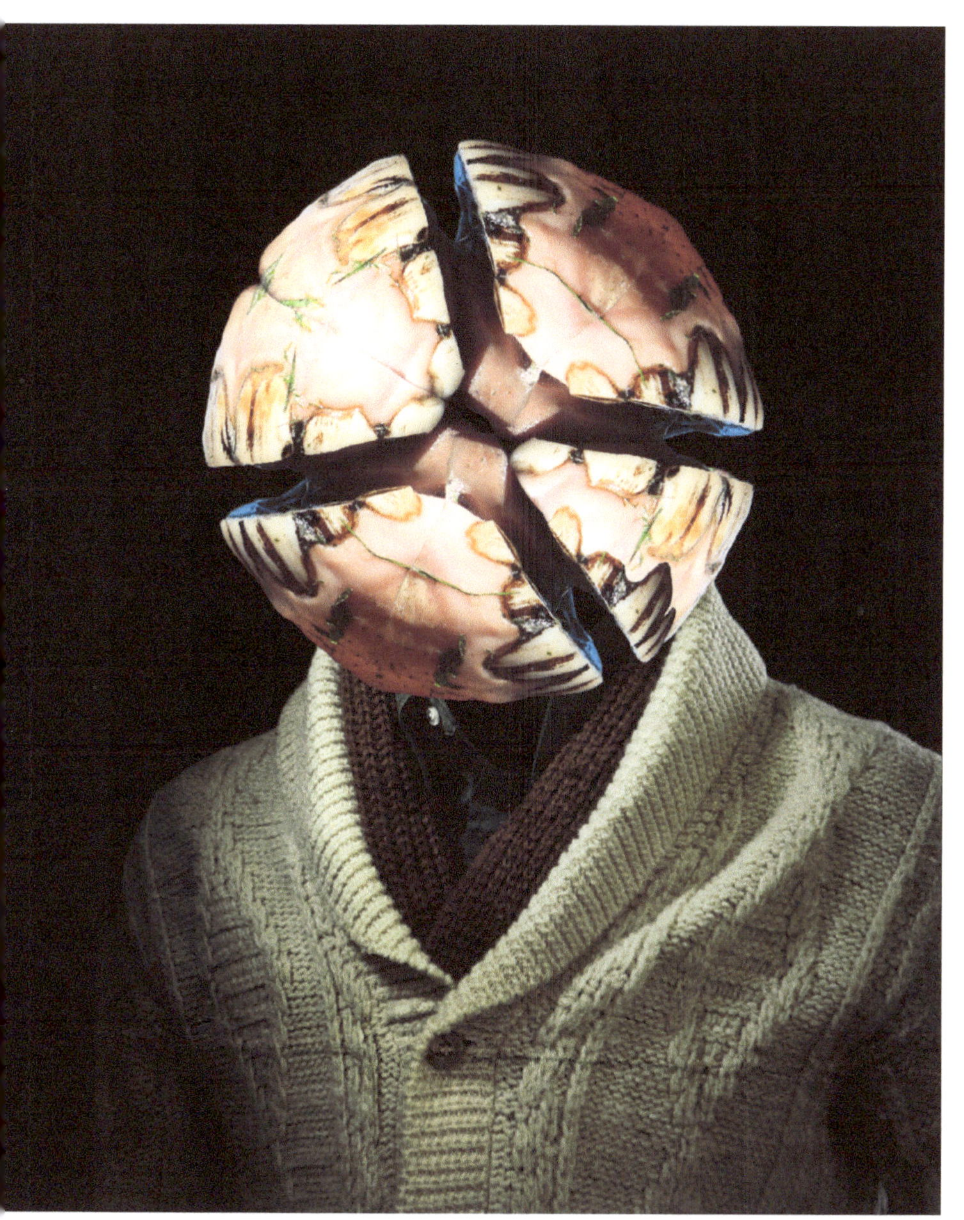

The Ruminator, 2023

The Nail Biter

tastes ...

soil trapped beneath a bell jar.
a loss of growth. the crimson flash
of a STOP sign shouting
its significance by the color of its urgency.
a resurrection
of boredom fed, again & again,
sized & shaped into perfection—misled.
the gnawing of a mindset, the chewing
of reasoning.
the bastard birth of anxiety
baptized in thick plunges of saliva
& insecurity.
the words of a mother's nagging,
& the memory of a memory
of polish remover never working.
a sunless growth of trapped animal instinct,
where one gnaws away
at a seized phantom limb,
manifested.

Contemplation

Enter the day by which I severed
the heads of seconds

as a tribute to my indecision,
dedicating their timely offerings

as my lifeblood in their eulogies.
That day, I left work early

without saying a word,
flooding as if tears could baptize me

in rejuvenation, as if salt could be
my drowning resurrection,

as if leaving were as visceral a need
as surviving.

That day, I searched for methods
by which death solves life's enigma.

Searched roadblock barriers & guardrails
in tire-hungry inches.

Searched my pupils cast
in kitchen-knife reflections.

Searched the intoxicating nebulas
of car exhaust, & considered the sacrifice

of teeth & tongue to dine on a bullet.
There are a thousand different ways to destroy

the human body, to crack the cage
of consciousness loose, to escape.

& my severed seconds piled
into the mass grave of an hour,

while life stumbled on
like a drunken god.

Living Will

If only I could take my life
by the sharp certainty of a blade,

& surgically sever the unspent seconds
as a parting gift signed *Anonymous*,

I'd pour them free to eager hands
with the innocence of apple juice arsenic,

& manifest the key to this cranium cage
to allow the beast its due.

No more attempts at senseless flight
with Dickinson's frayed feathers.[3]

No more attempts to snatch the tune
from the wordless morning bird.

I'd prescribe myself a final act
of justifiable violence,

carving portions of fruitful parts
from a life wasted in idle wander.

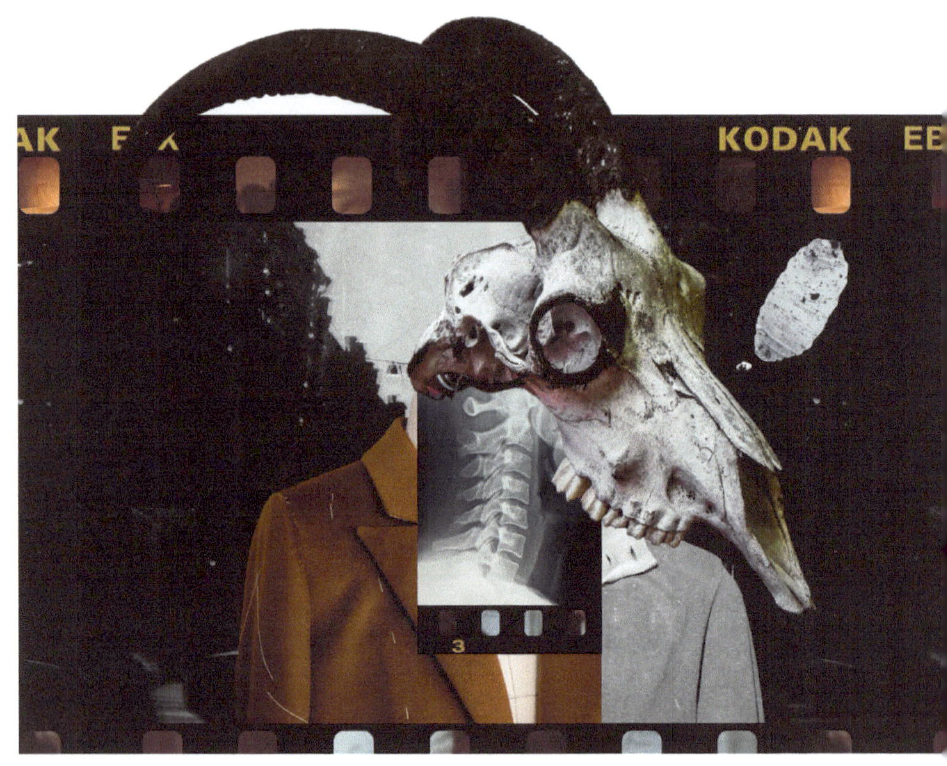

Dead Air, 2023

Transmission of Dead Air

What I could never prepare for
was the separation of emotion,

& with it, the dissociation
of everything coupled soundly

between it. Indifference
becomes the smallest distance

to life's final destination.
A closely clipped fingernail's width

of space presumed uncharted, despite all
my contrary maps previously constructed.

I'm a cartographer retracing a border
inked onto the paper.

A border as thick as telephone wire
transmitting dead air

to the living still connected.
Dead air once split the distance

between my indifference & a blade
in a house of recollection I unwillingly revisit.

Where creaking floorboards sound
like the snapping prongs of a ribcage,

& with it, a natural translation
to a wordless language.

Where the rotting doorway
of the living room whispers

a windowless breeze,
deflating like the stomach

of a rupturing carcass squeezed
by desert heat.

Where an armchair pressing paling
crimson from its fabric beckons

with protruding guts of stuffing
& springs. Where I can sink

into the rat-gnawed cavity
of the cushion,

tuning eyes to waves of glowing
pixelated static,

irises melting into the flickering
television prison,

while I repeatedly fail
to feel anything—at all.

Ghost Machine

inertia spirit agitated by mechanical moments,
gutting gears to smoke-screen self-purpose's blur.
blue-screened but masked in mechanisms of the living.
backfiring to breakdowns & seeping soundlessly in a world of oil.

float through the sludge of a black gravity,
a never-ending situation compounding,
eroding *tick-tock-ticks* to soil sleep.
voice your questions to the dark
& taste the hammering
hum of static—

crescendoing
like a tempered dial
beneath the weight of wattage.

Morbid Curiosity

I once had a friend ask me,
out of morbid curiosity,
which method of death I would prefer
if given an option.

"Would you rather be ignited
in vibrant shades of autumn orange & gold
with some potent-smelling gasoline
& the all-consuming blaze
of an innocent torch?"

"Or perhaps you'd prefer a bullet to the brain?
One that twists & turns & dances freely.
One that combines flesh & bone
& your exquisite gray matter
into a violently beautiful, artistically suicidal
array of pure self-destruction."

But before my friend could deliver a final option,
I delivered one of my own.

Spitting the toxic venom from the tip of my tongue,
& deciphering the whispers gracefully ushering me
to the confines of my gravely home,
I delivered my own option
in transparently emotionless monotone.

"I would prefer to drown," I said.

"I would prefer to submerge myself
beneath gentle, yet unforgiving waters.
Waters that perfectly blend
my numerous sins & endless convictions,

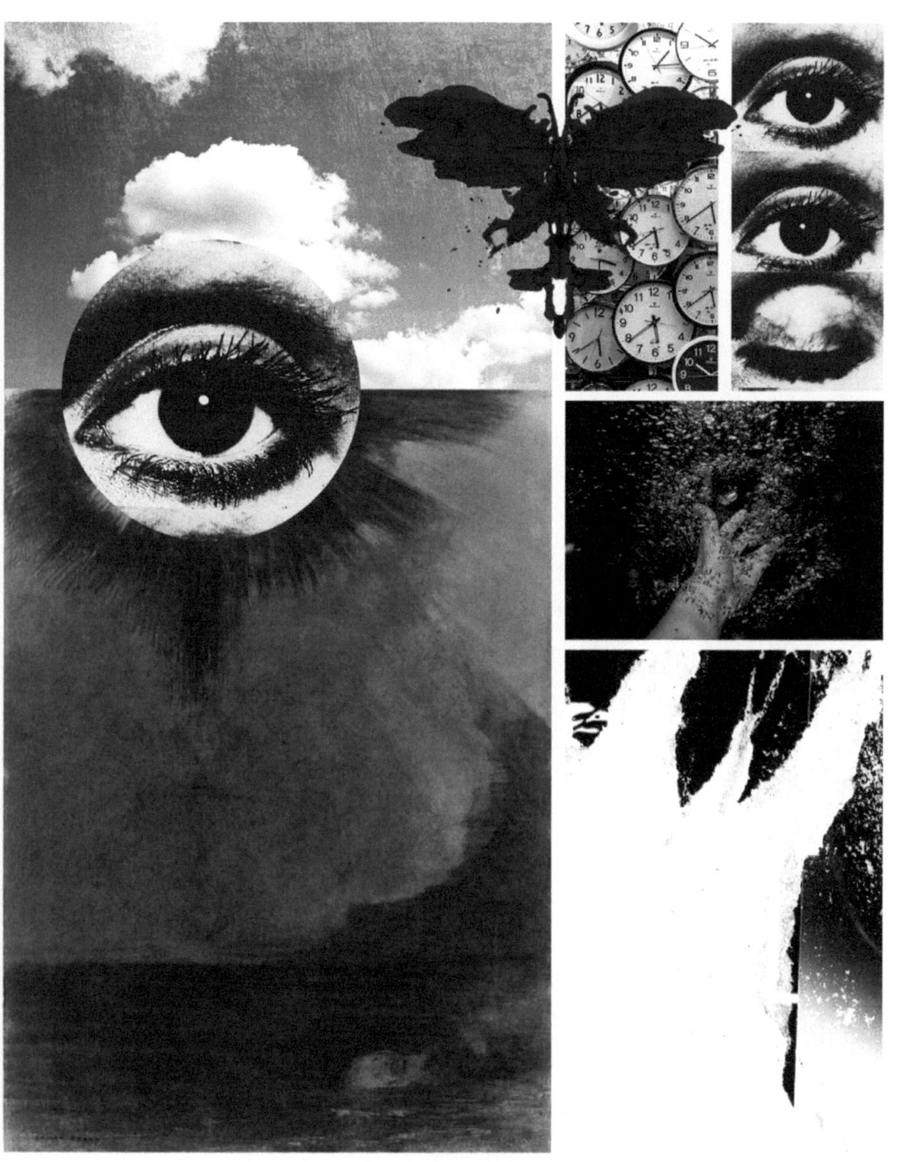

Drowning in the Ink of Oblivion, 2022

my every moment of cowardly indecision,
my fears & failed ambitions
into an intoxicating cocktail which
I ingest & never awake from."

"I would prefer to perfectly match,
in the last ten seconds of my life,
the same suffocating pressure
felt within my chest,
the same breathless composure
felt within my lungs,
the same incurable hopelessness
felt within my heart
as I have experienced in nearly
every moment of my waking life."

"& I would prefer, with my last shallow breath,
to have pleasant memories flash within my eyelids,
just to embrace, one final time,
what true happiness felt like."

Speechless silence filled the air,
fading to deafening ambience,
as my friend's throat failed to clear,
as my friend's disabled vocal cords
failed to produce a string of words
that didn't dress themselves up as
sentence fragments.

As words cautiously escaped from the corners
of my friend's expressionless lips,
I produced a worn, white handkerchief
& gently dabbed at the toxic venom
that had spewed from my mouth.

Then I began to speak again.

"I would prefer to drown, my friend,
for to drown is not foreign to me, nor
is the suffocating nature of its affliction.
& even in death, it appears
I would rather not drift outside
the self-securing confines of
my comfort zone."

Indigo

The gravest sound does not reach past
the mouth of a river. It curves around
its indigo lips, barely touches, dissipates.
Anybody singing in dirges from its depths
will never hear their tune reverberate,
wet off the surface. The light will never
touch their face. How does one live
beneath the water—blue-faced—
& yet, not drown? By some sort of
anatomical magic? Or the crow's curse?
Tell me how a dying mind imagines a living
hope, or a rescue, or a disembodied
hand that breaks through.

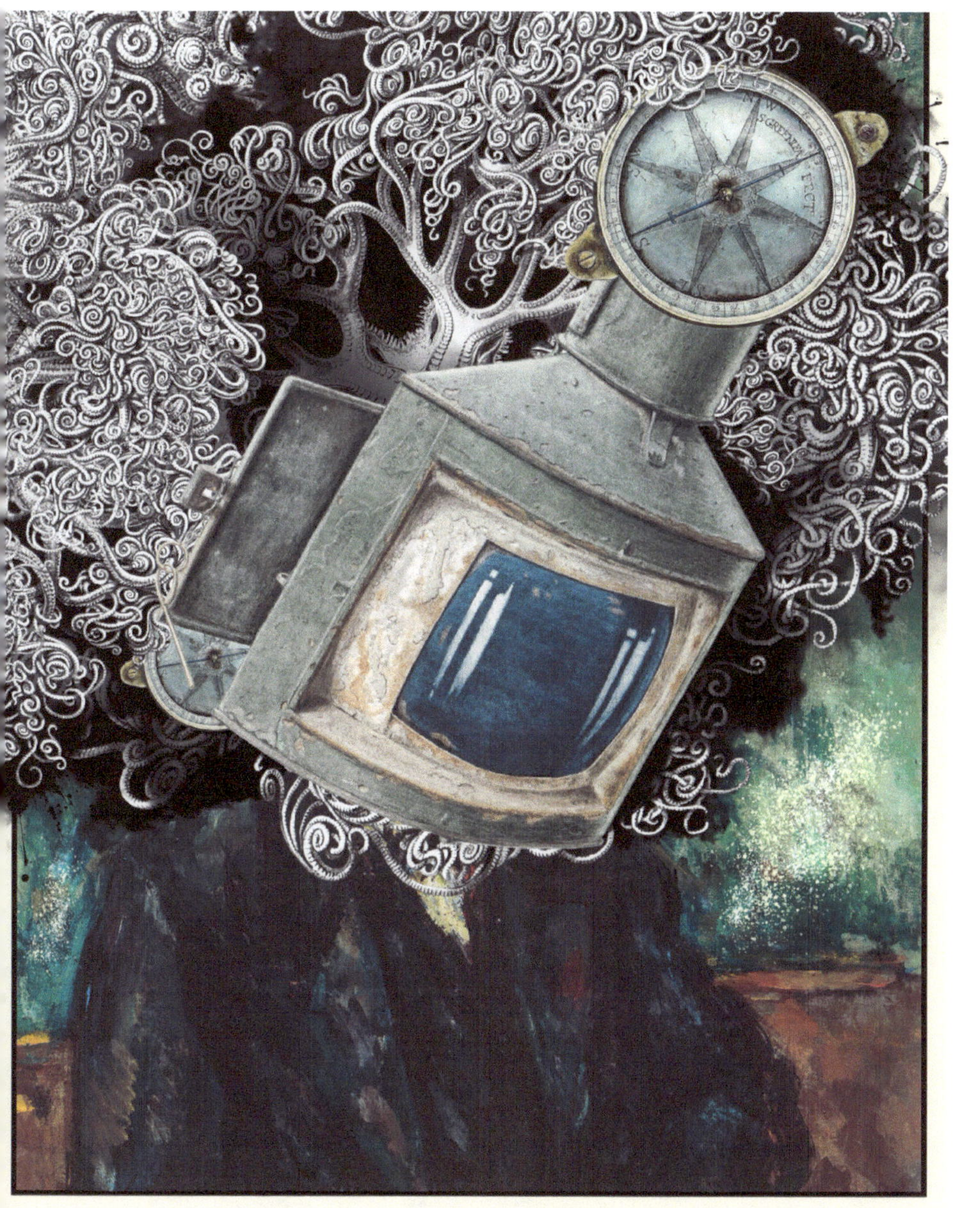

The Cranium Cage, 2024

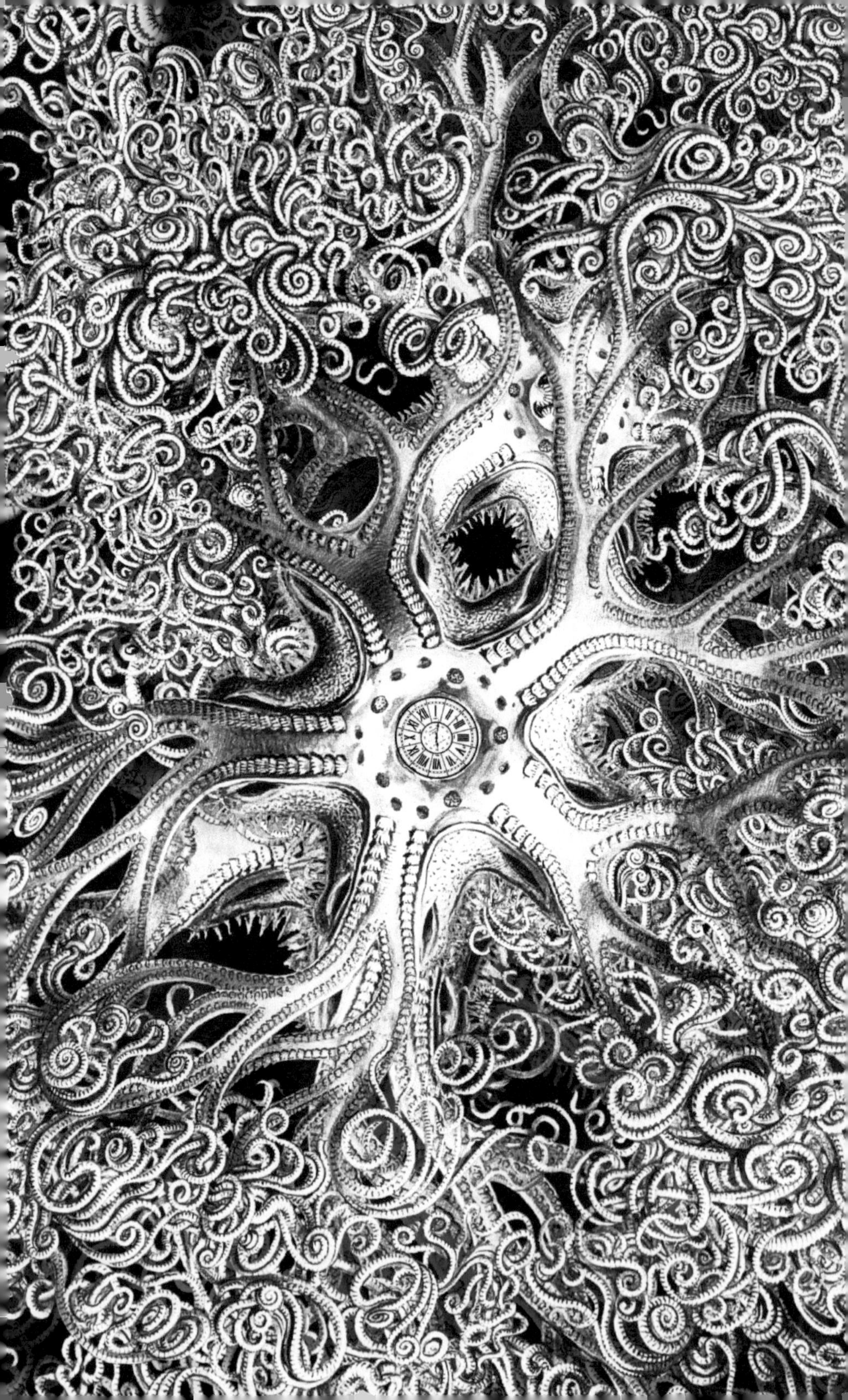

II

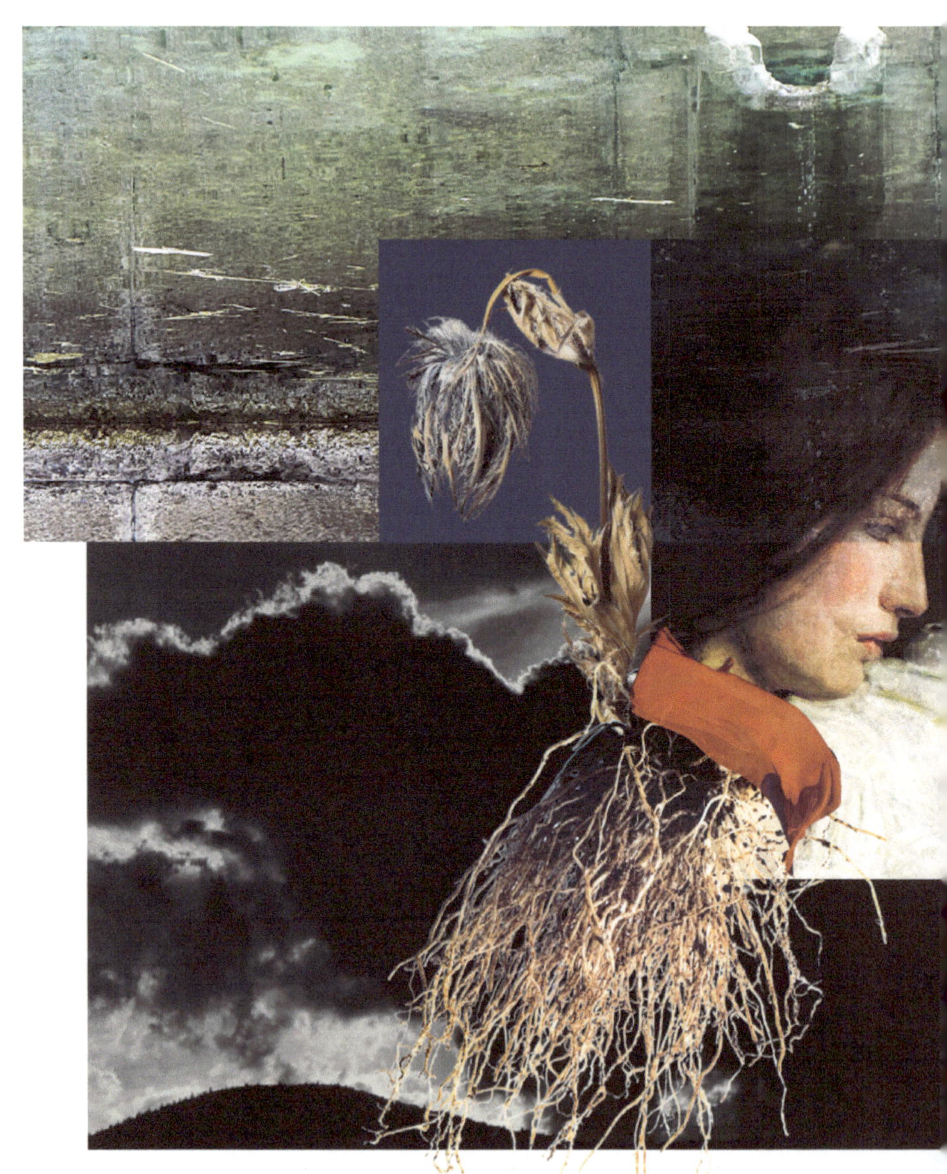

Withered, 2021

Contagion

The twelve steps to the receptionist span
twelve miles, each a reverse-moving walkway
of carpet trapping my feet in stationary motion.

I'm fifty minutes early after skipping seconds
from the driver's seat, but she is not as surprised
as I am to see me. She slides the surgical mask

of plexiglass to the right, provokes the dull tooth
of her clipboard to lock my paperwork in a perpetual
bite, & politely gestures me towards a seat, stating

that I will be seen shortly. The surgical mask
is slid back, & I see in the quarantined aftermath
that she collects seashells. Moonshells, conchs,

cross-barred venuses. Perhaps what we choose
to collect is what we wish to reclaim,
& our dying echoes of memory lay

living inside these hollow items to soothe
our souls. I face the furnished fullness
of an empty room, & silently hope she's okay.

A crimson armchair beckons me from beyond
row after row of vomit-colored green, as each seat
spreads an illness infecting the nearby paintings

inside their half-glass houses. Restless frames
shift in fever dreams to whichever side is facing me,
glaring in swollen hunger as the walls themselves

are incessantly swallowed. I'm squeezed to the back
of this brute throat, a sunken lump left
tongue-pressed against the off-color back wall,

waiting for the moment when I'm regurgitated
to the front again, where I will slip from this room
like thick phlegm only to be collected softly in

the tissue of my diagnosis: *clinical depression.*
& again, I will visit here, wrung out into a seat,
reeking of yesterday's Cabernet

& today's sobering nausea, careful to avoid
the crimson armchair, knowing there's a desire
there better left unspoken, a desire

to be the color of the fabric & choosing
nothing but the reassurance of my sickness
to sink myself into, hoping as the receptionist

continues to collect more patients
& more seashells, that she will remain
unaffected inside her half-glass house.

Session One

He asks for me to start
from the beginning, to remember

when the symptoms first occurred,
& my mind chews on the memory

of my bill-beaten mother explaining
to me patiently the persistence of absence,

& how it bears the featureless face
of my father.

I think of explaining to him
that absence never leaves

the same way
by which it came.

It lingers
by the oak archway of childhood

& invites in more guests
until the ground floor caves in.

To remember childhood then
becomes a memory of headcounts,

& recollection never regards
limits of maximum capacity.

I remember the heavy thuds
of mechanic boots spitting

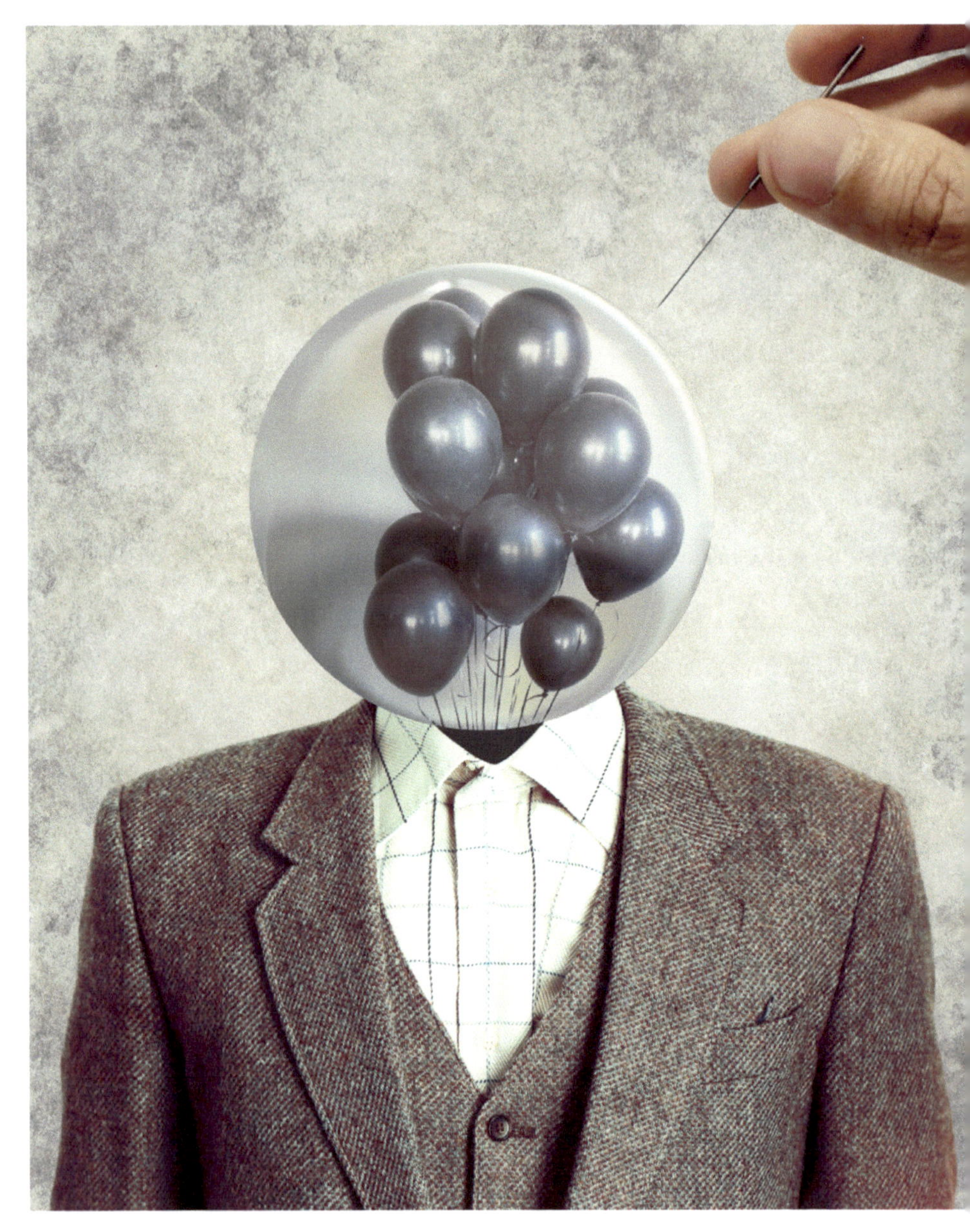

Session One, 2023

a cyclone of animated
roadrunner dust,

as the syllables of *father*
slipped back

beneath my tongue.
I remember the taste

of metallic, my blood birthing
guiltiness into my broken mouth,

as I brawled against a schoolyard
of my own unwanted inheritance.

I remember the uncanny shift
of the entire world falling

perpetually off its axis
when my father met me.

He introduced me
like an untrustworthy stray dog

to his proud purebred family.
He introduced me

as if my presence possessed
an expiration date:

two weeks until I became
spoiled milk discarded

in the drain of his unwanted
history.

Left spiraling, spiraling,
spiraling until I subtly slipped

eons into this half-insured hour,
& sank

into the luminous crow color
of tar-thick bubbling ink,

watching as it ballooned
& burst from my thoughts

as Rorschach blots, decorating
white wallpapered emptiness,

all while leaving
a myriad of reasons

for the silence in the room
to be analyzed.

What I'm Made of

kerosene thinking & stillborn dreams,
red-eyed reflections & blue-faced realities,
a total eclipse, stuck in stasis—
my faulty wiring.

a film reel projector on fire & flapping,
a future of smoke screen emissions from musing,
or the sputtering wings of a bluebird—
framed & shot.

tombs of romance rot, Rorschach blots,
miscalculated connections;
impermanence-mentality downs
& deadbeat-dad mad dashes,
childhood trailer-home traumas
& countless rejections.

an atlas called *The Noonday Demon* dissected—
snip-snapped, broken down.
the hues of Sexton's "Yellow" driving
bellyfuls of doubt.+
fingernail chewings in fistfuls—
my burial grounds.

my every subconscious constraint unbound:
black pages parading undetected,
flowing & flowing & flowing in a literary abyss.

Pendulum Possession

life remembered as lingering loss

plight pendulum's a like heavy loss

plight of hanging on: an ever-thinning thread

[5]clock Dali's by cursed, mortal coiled thread

clock forever melting, clock coldly perpetuating

mind of sways swift memory's perpetuating

mind swinging as if possessed

stabilize cannot I, possessed

Another Round

"Stabilize," says my therapist
as I bar reality & split,
dashing idly before
suspending between self
& destruction.

"Reframe," he adds,
& amber curvatures draw me in,
where bottle-by-bottle deductions shape
a starving pain
weightless.

"Exhale,"
he grounds in brevity,
but I seem only to float ...

to where sips serve confidence
& all loss aversion folds.
By tipsy bluffs, directionless,
I let my compass circle.

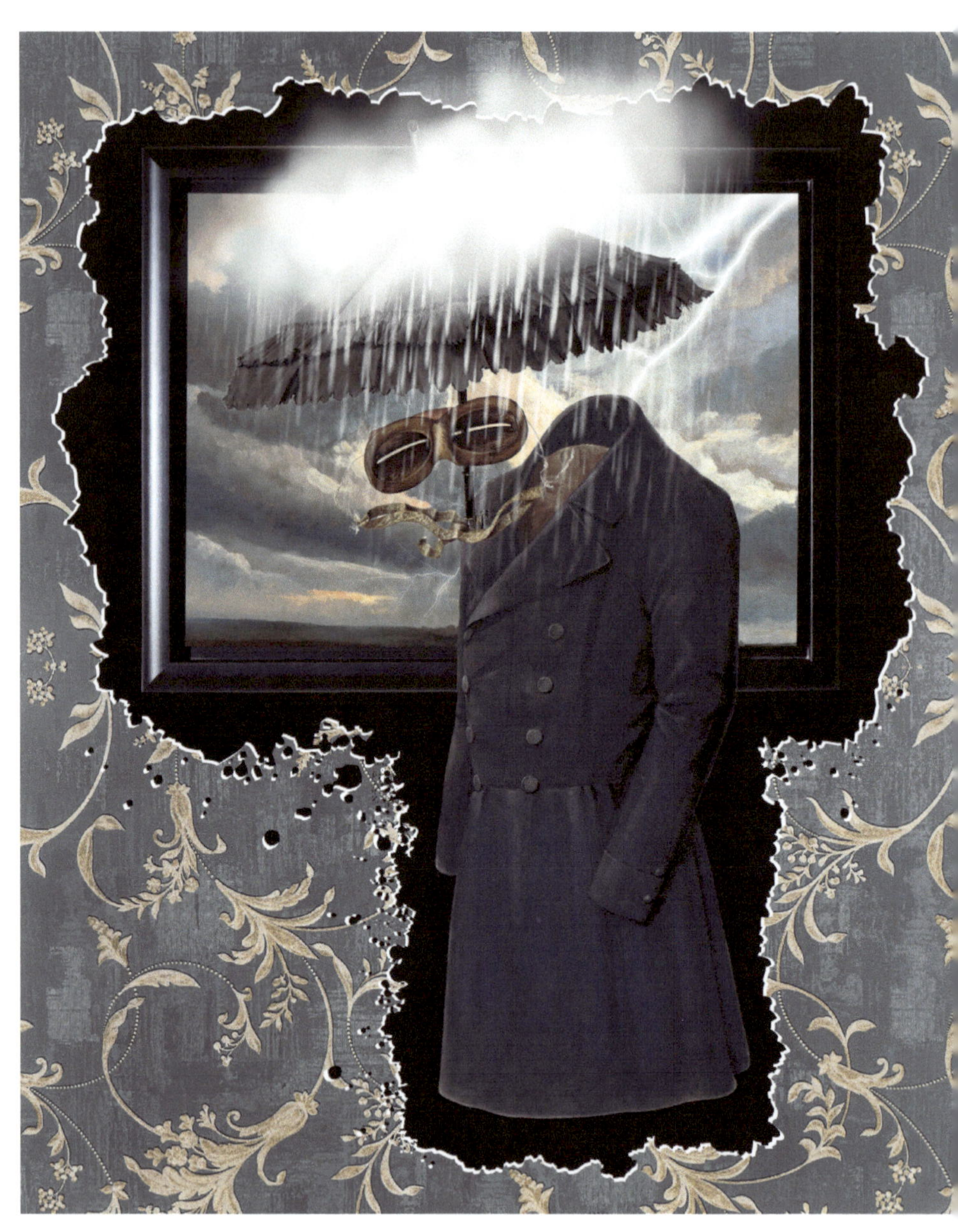

Dissolve, 2024

Dissolve

My 20/20 tunnel vision is a black & blue
fist through white sheetrock, then removed.
No panoramic views.
My mind brews bitterness as if cauldron-bound,
as if knuckle-writing *FUCK THIS* in men's stalls
around the city – in bloody symbology –
defines me by some savage rationality. It does,
presently: intoxicated. But what about the next?
What mental projection will I follow? What manifestation
of sorrow, of myself, through shapeshifting
inanimate objects into scenes of unabashed violence
will I sink fists through? By which moment
is my identity not defined by film reels of lost lives
& memories? By which frame does the vertebrae
of my monochrome mind break? By which crack carving
acceptance into memory's cinematic sequence
rolls reality's dark picture technicolor for a change of cast?

Captured

Unlocked, my apartment vacant
without her in it,
my confined cranium

squeaks open its hinges,
revealing a skeleton
shoebox of recollection:

anniversary & birthday cards, husks
of movie stubs,
little scraps of shriveled letters,

photographs compiled together
like bodies left
huddling for warmth.

These captured scenes are replaying,
decaying,
disembodying its featured audience

into cold,
hollow loops
of remembrance refuse

in a dilapidated theater
with ticket torn
for one.

Afterimages of her presence
hoard my present. & I scurry away
to strike off the lights.

But my vision succumbs to this door
                                        slammed shut—
like a rodent trapped by a copper mouth.

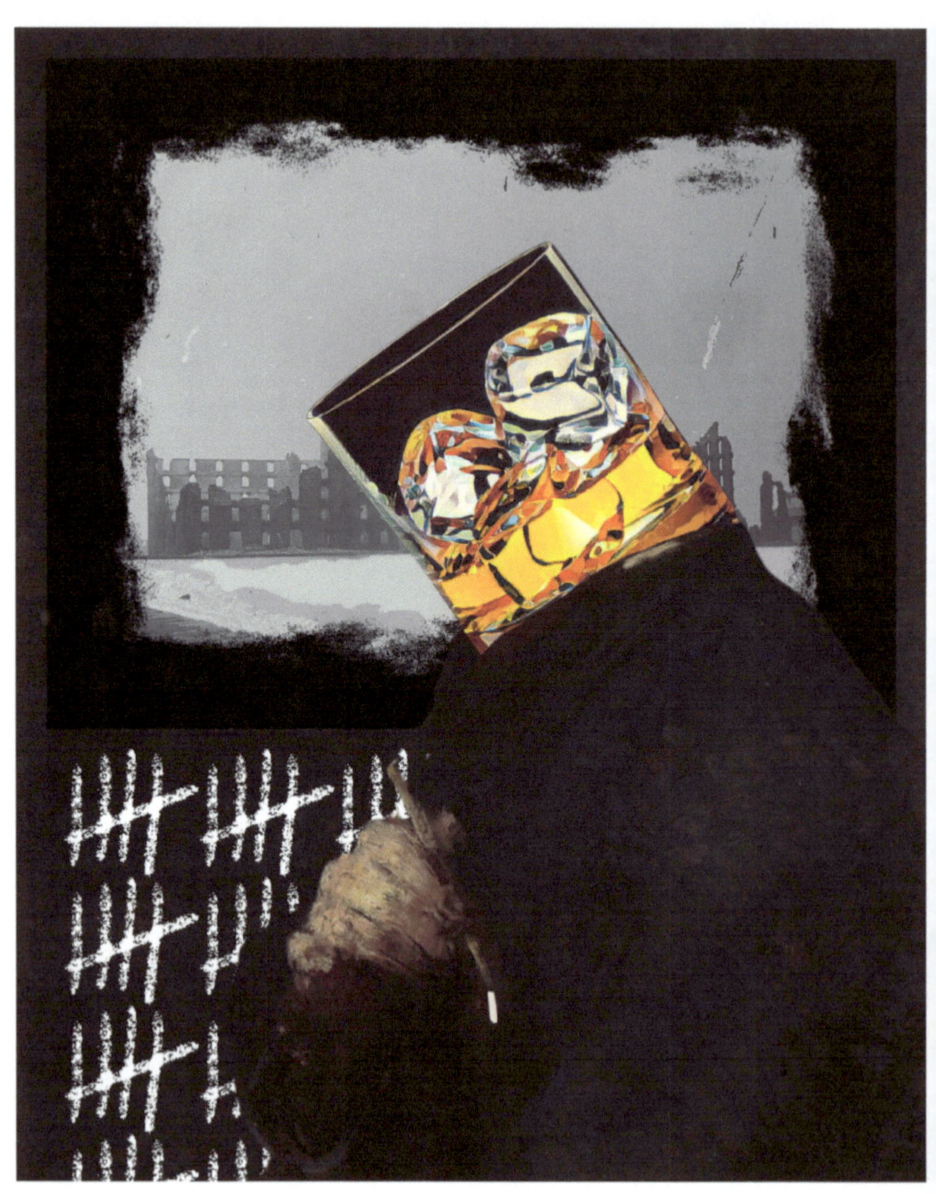

Habitual Grief, 2023

Like a Shadow Trailing Your Years

How long must a longing trail?
My hunger looms like a wolfish shadow,
gutting memories of someone else.

Stretch the past's persistence like intestinal tract,
attempt to tear it with trembling hands,
or surgically, scissor snip it.
Its mortal coil lies
wrapped in immortality.

What deep rest it must seek,
hopelessly. The hollowing ache
of its own loitering sickening
bars & back alleys across the city.

Everything evacuates from the nooks
& crannies of my liquored stomach.
My mind stalks ...
Pounces!
Feasts as if nothing happened.

Maybes & Prescribed Remedies

"See you tomorrow" has become more question
than statement, more *maybe* than *definitely*.

Lately, I often wonder which melting day
will solidify into the bullet night chambers.

Which disgruntled today
will murder tomorrow?

Which teetering second will shift its weight
to the wrong side of life & death?

Plato spoke of this condition
of being human, that we all must balance

in a state of in-betweenness.
He called it metaxis.

Rationality & irrationality. Love
& hate. Time & eternity. Life & death.

If Plato is correct,
then how do you fix an imbalance?

My therapist suggests antidepressants.
A pill, some sharp chemical cutlery

built to carve out the peach pits of rot
clinging to the tender flesh of my thoughts.

But I believed each encapsulated blade
would sculpt me dull, somehow.

Somehow, each white-knight pill
would turn opponent,

reshape the fragile seeds
of my artistry

into nothing but wastelands
& ruin. To bring forth oceans

of serotonin to drain bone-dry—
would seal me in the plastic womb

that birthed it.
I'm fine

with wondering which melting day
will solidify into the bullet night chambers,

if starry nights still ingrain flashes
of resilience in me like the explosions

lit by painters & poets. Perhaps that itself
is some sort of balance struck—

as I embrace the dying words
of Vincent.[6]

Carved Captive

Shadow-dancing with my melancholy master,
I seek solace in a shelter of sawdust dreams.
In this negative space, the living moments I trace,
In their luminous but dying light,
Thread pulls to my past like puppetry,
Manifest me with these strings attached.

Questions chew my wooden mouth to splinters.
My vision skewered by each *why* delivered.
Ventriloquist my lips with imitated existence,
Sway my languid limbs,
But I'm stuck to the ruin of my own undoing.

Carved to be captive, spiraling in suspension,
Grain against grain, I thin from my faults.
Carved to be captive, curtain-pull this production,
As the puppeteer commandeers his strung-out star.

Discarded like a prop in despondency,
Stage shrouded in the safety of darkness,
Contortions of uncanny accordions
Straighten to silence—
Where, in a hollowed hell, I obsessively piece
Fragments of remembered life,
Reflecting in kaleidoscope fashion
Faint traces of happiness—
Before they're smashed.

Carved to be captive, spiraling in suspension,
Grain against grain, I thin from my faults.
Carved to be captive, curtain-pull this production,
As the puppeteer commandeers his strung-out star.

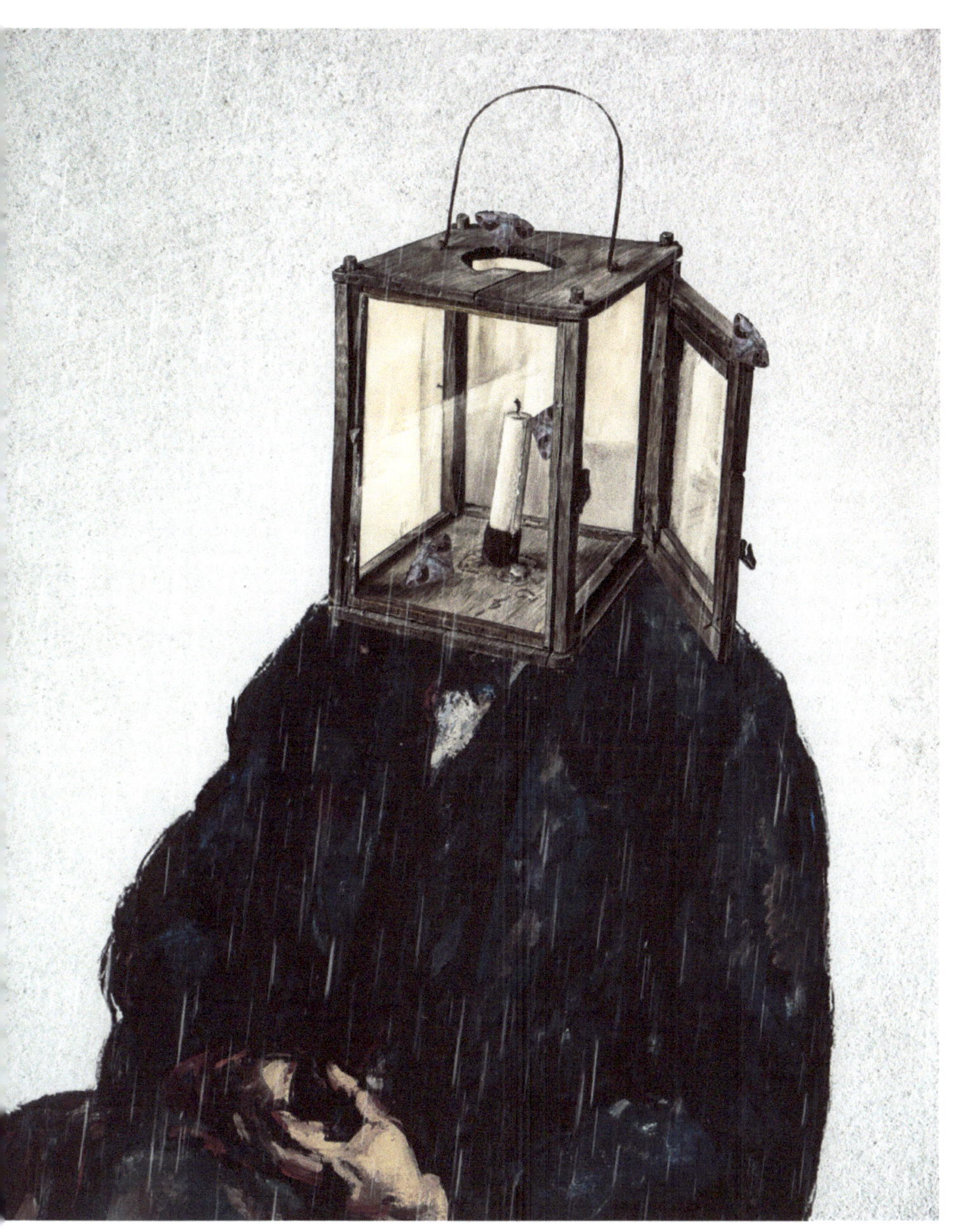

Robbed of Light, 2024

I have killed the cricket of reason
With the hammer of rumination.
My present: poverty-stricken,
Robbed of light.

I have killed the cricket of reason
With the hammer of rumination.
But ethereal chirps persist, persuade,
Ignite.[7]

This Hell, My Home, Splinters My Mind Frame

& every bone in my verbs is misplaced, contorting from a lifetime of misguided exorcism. Brown bile, projectile vomiting, the drunken drowning of memories & insecurities of a near-thirty-year-old man. Am I the stumbling, stuttering faith within a battling priest? Or the unholy manifestation of my own ill-kept demons? Tell me ... Tell me to rest. To rest in the solace of fatigue, not existentially exhausted, but tired like a laboring man no longer spending wages drinking away the seasons. No longer spending numbered days numb in the face of it all, but smiling as if life finally means something. As if all my clocks have struck the same hour of peace in infinite understanding. As if the illusion is a lifetime holding. As if the illusion is no longer an illusion, & I have conquered my fear of dissolving. As if forward movement is prayer, is confession, is waking hope. & every bone in my verbs has reset.

Rise

In the depths of a dream,
I plunge—

my pruned digits into
the sun & squeeze,

totalize its sweet shine
& taste honey mead,

dissect a light buzz
with a surgeon's tongue,

excise some orange slices
with a scalpel,

& drip-feed their seeds
to ignite the shadows

of my ruined lives towering
like tombstones,

until sunflowers pry forth
like green fingertips

to clip away dense clouds
of gray.

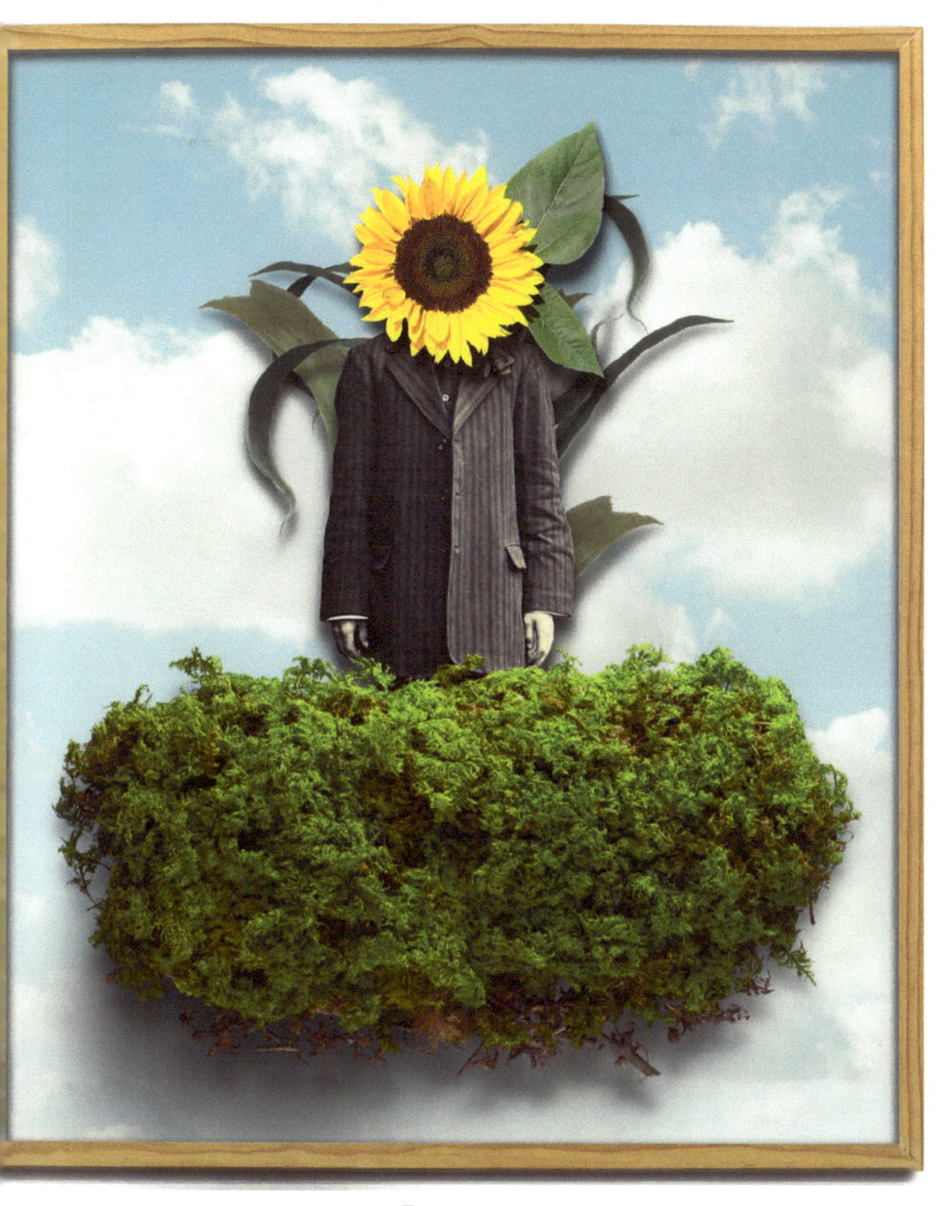

Rise, 2022

Moving

I awake to an empty master
bedroom in 115, flesh freezing
to suit the bone-bare walls
& freshly carved cavities
of closets, warmth stolen
by each greedy little hand
on the carpet, where bodies
of ascending dust pass
like raptured souls to greet
their eternal morning.

March's outpouring optimism
baptizes me from a blindless window,
conducting silent sermons
of self-forgiveness that only leave me
feeling nauseous.

She loved me here—
once.

She, my olive tree, uprooted,
like our dreams: a clementine seedling,
an oak meadow rustling to life ...
now only soiled hands rest soundly
by my side.

I crack a desert to catch water
in a hazel eye,
to cleanse my meeting with dismay
in this aftermath mirage,
to flood these leaves & try & leave
a tidy home in a hoarder's mind.

I sweep the floors, scrub the walls,
vacuum the rugs, & before
locking the door—

I look back ...
                    one
                        last
                            time.

Remedial Flight

It made me inhospitable: my need
for a remedy rattling to rumination,

buzzed from a bottle yielding a nectar
of numbness, honeycombed with sinkholes

in a worming mind of self-destruction.
My own growth rotting, I heard hums

of an isolating darkness deep within
my perspective forest, panoramic chaos

breeding insects for my future
of ghost trees. What attempts I carve

against this deadening in carbon-
copy days as dull as crinkled cardboard,

the sheer ache of existence ingrained
like tree rings embedded in my throat,

choking down my aging as each paperback
passerby hurries to finish their chapter,

the frenzy of their handwritten vitality
lost to me, my stagnation a crumpling

of blank pages, & I wonder ...
what life rooted in them, dried up in me?

What attempts I nurture,
like spawn from the earth, to cure myself,

bound to books like glue to feathers,
or a pre-med, sleep-deprived student.

No rest; no solace; no hope. Never-
theless, I thought of remedial flight.

What marvels that sky must hold that I can-
not touch—yet I attempt,

sight dizzy from ascending height
in a perpetual fall.

Conjuring the Overlooked

They don't arrive quite as I imagined,
my epiphanic moments, clarity dissolving
vast valleys of fog, stray light piercing
through the darkness, or *glimmers*,
as my therapist thoughtfully calls them.

Seized moments of scorching white,
joy-thick & true, like burning color
reaching through life's suffering
to greet you, I welcome their imprint
on my mind like a kiss of eternal sunshine.

Underlying, undying, as powerful as King's shining,[8]
in a psychic surge illuminating lands of shadow,
glimmers are sudden floodlights searching
past my living deaths.

Their circulating cycles act like lighthouses,
navigating vitality across my rigor mortis surface,
highlighting my pale face to beckon blood back
into its place—with golden grace.

Yet rumination breeds a new tarnish,
for how long have I walked this world haunted,
veil-draped & sullen,
hunted by habitual animal roars
as my beast reduces me
to nothing?

Best to kill that question
by reflecting
in a shelter of silver.

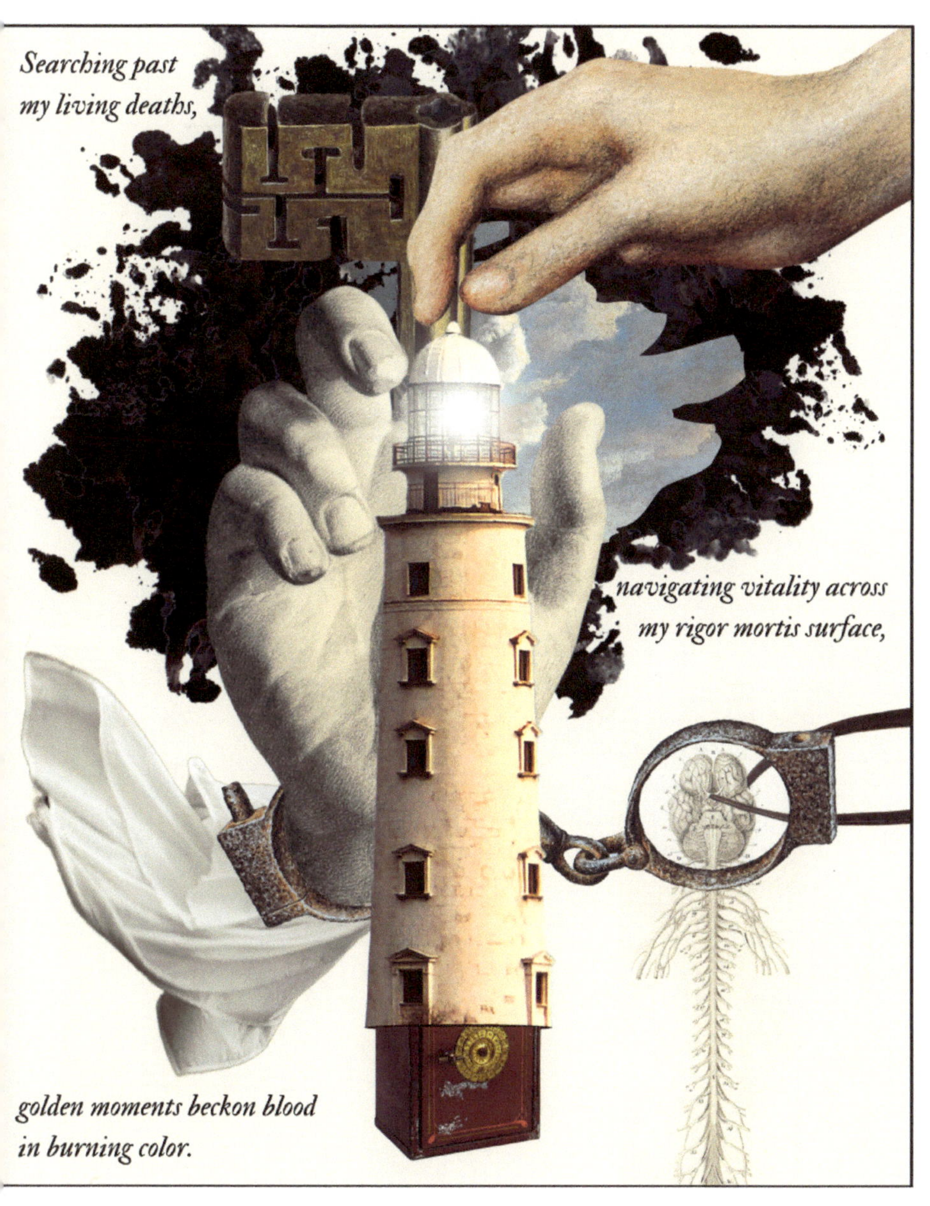

Beckoning Vitality, 2024

To humor my brooding like a hedge maze deprived
of exits, devoid of answers, paralyzed
in its questions, its frozen wonders, in a sun-starved
maddening obsession, that would be my murder
of sense & self.

Glimmers are a source of my re-embodiment;

(beyond a head
that plays host
to a hotel of horrors:
fitting rooms
with the flesh
of my energy,
responding
by reanimating
memory,
feeding walls
with my living
blood)

they help me vanish
back into the present.
& reinforced like a séance of sorts
by the willful reassurance of my therapist,
such hope seeps in through this ushering summons
to life.

My Final Act

is to break from my carousel of ruin
to stable freedom like wild horses;

is to ghostwrite the spell to a golden time,
to make it mine,
alchemize a mind-of-ease paradise,
(plagiarized?)
until these written words of amber break
my daily beer bottles,
releasing color like stained glass shattering
in cathedrals
& altering the weight of my grayscale,
as a new morning lights my temples;

is to leave starved my corrupted machine,
a page-hungry parasite of narrative gnawing,
to proofread perspective & host my reality
with all-new edits;

is to question the depths of my own gradient,
filter transparency through the black
of tangled film,
to splice and re-spool this shadow reel
under the guidance of scene-set acceptance,
director's cut manifested to noncritical analysis,
the viewing: the audience: my singular admission;
my present casting one last final applause—
to curtain the "could have been," "would have been"
to what never was;

is to leave my hibernation in chthonic darkness,
shelter self from the persuasion of my sunken place,

to cave the frantic flight impulses
condemning me to crushing caution
against all therapeutic responses
to my undermining.

is an underlying yearning for yet another final act,
my anticipatory wish rippling
through a black water well,
submerging my silver for an honorable exchange:
to silence my inclinations to leave the stage.

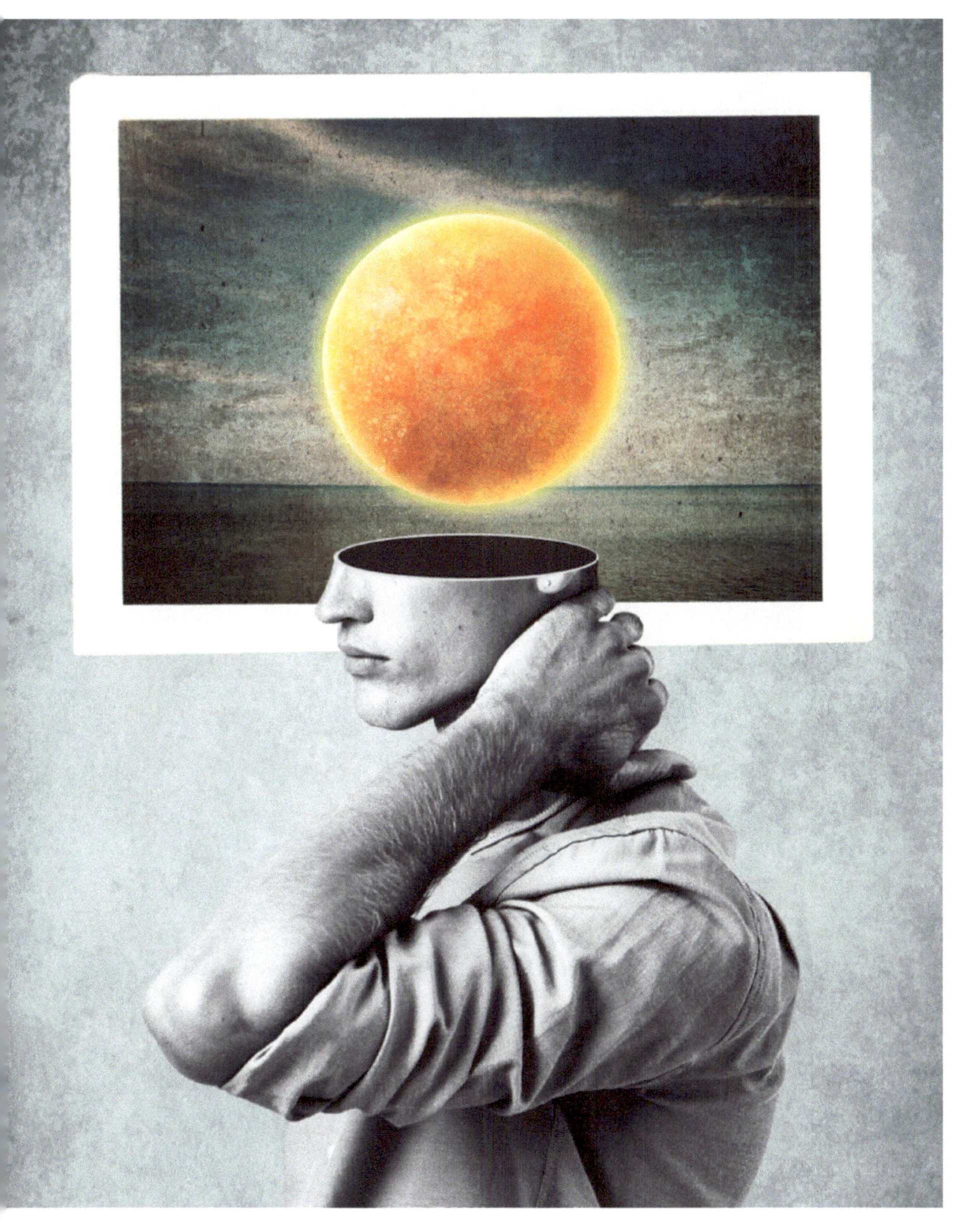

Confidence, 2022

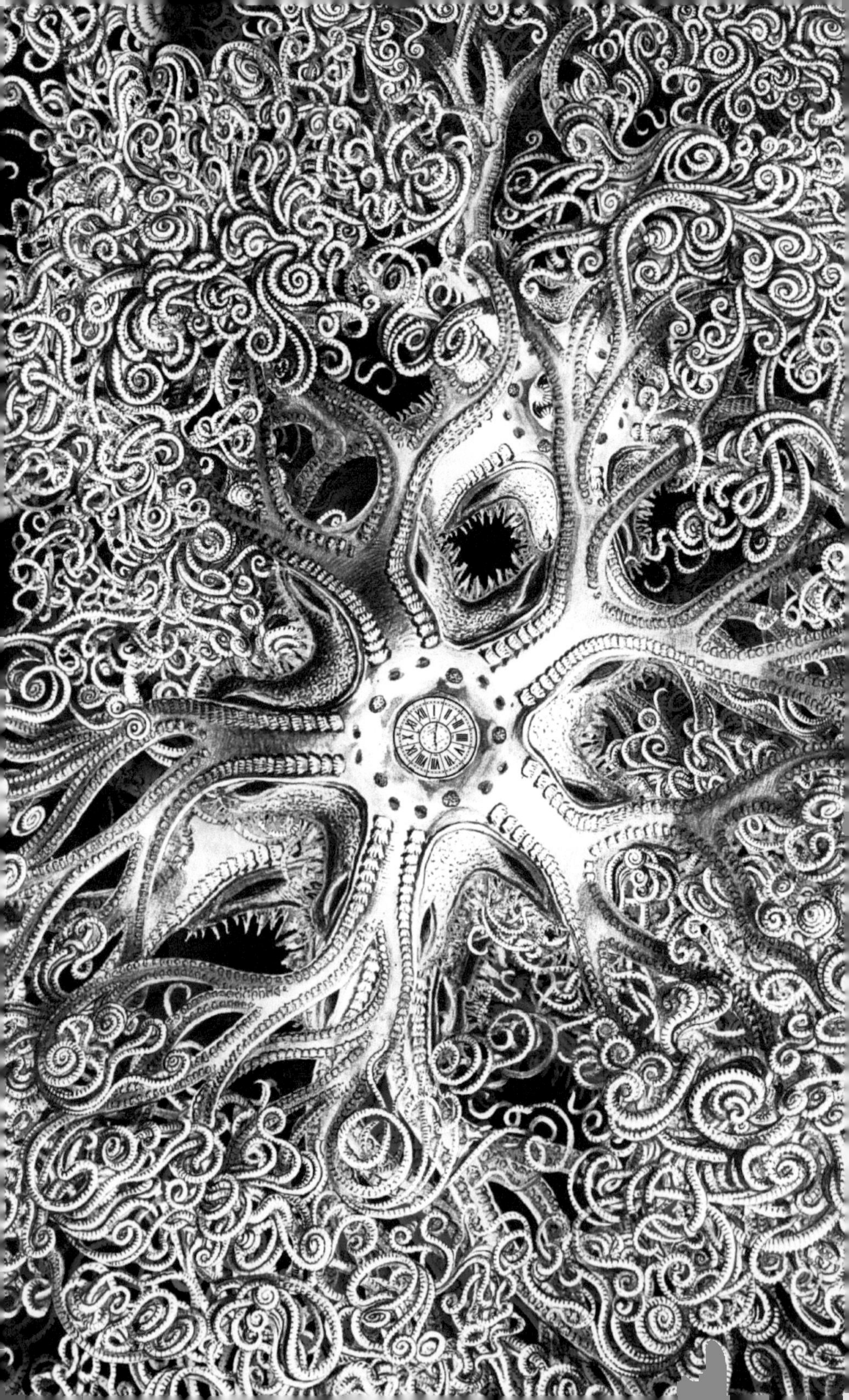

Notes

1) "From the Mouths of Shadows" – "*Larghetto,*" the title of the musical piece used in this collage artwork, is an Italian musical term for "slightly slow" or "a little slower." It is usually played at a tempo of sixty beats per minute, drawing comparisons to a resting heart rate, and invites a sense of introspection through its restrained sense of motion. Below "*Larghetto,*" the subtitle "*ma non molto passione*" translates to "but not much passion," and its inclusion was meant to expand upon the melancholic grace displayed within this piece.

2) "Savior Complex" – The lines "*Thou art the Creator of all things, visible & invisible ...*" and "*From the snares of the devil, deliver us ...*" are excerpts from the "Exorcism Prayer of St. Michael the Archangel."

3) "Living Will" – The lines "No more attempts at senseless flight with Dickinson's frayed feathers. No more attempts to snatch the tune from the wordless morning bird" are in reference to the first stanza of Emily Dickinson's poem, "'Hope' is the thing with feathers."

4) "What I'm Made of" – The line "An atlas called *The Noonday Demon* dissected—snip-snapped, broken down" is in reference to the book *The Noonday Demon: An Atlas of Depression* by Andrew Solomon. Also, the line "the hues of Sexton's *Yellow* driving bellyfuls of doubt" is a reference to the poem "Yellow" by Anne Sexton, specifically addressing her ending line, "we'll go on won't we?"

5) "Pendulum Possession" – The line "clock Dali's by cursed," meant to be read backwards as "cursed by Dali's clock," is in reference to the melting clocks seen in Salvador Dali's painting, "The Persistence of Memory." Through my own interpretation, his melting clocks demonstrate how memory is not restricted by the sharp, calculated hands of time, nor the intricate devices mankind utilizes to "contain" time. Memory can melt past into present, present into future, and by doing so, seeps into timelessness and can solidify into rumination.

6) "Maybes & Prescribed Remedies" – The line "as I embrace the dying words of Vincent" is in reference to Vincent van Gogh's dying words: "The sadness will last forever."

7) "Carved Captive" – The lines "I have killed the cricket of reason with the hammer of rumination. But ethereal chirps persist, persuade, ignite" are a reference to *The Adventures of Pinocchio* by Carlo Collodi. In the book, Pinocchio accidentally kills the Talking Cricket by throwing a hammer at it in a fit of fury. The Talking Cricket appears later in the story as a ghost to continue advising Pinocchio on his adventures.

8) "Conjuring the Overlooked" – The line "Underlying, undying, as powerful as King's shining" is a reference to Stephen King's horror novel, *The Shining*, specifically the powerful psychic abilities Danny Torrance and Dick Hallorann possess. There are other nods to *The Shining* seen throughout this poem as well, including the line " ... a hedge maze deprived of exits, devoid of answers, paralyzed in its questions, its frozen wonders, in a sun-starved maddening obsession, that would be my murder of sense & self," which relates to the full-blown madness of lead character Jack Torrance, who winds up lost and frozen in the hotel's hedge maze in one of the last – and arguably, most memorable – scenes in Stanley Kubrick's film adaption. The poem's title itself, "Conjuring the Overlooked," is a play on the historic resort that served as the primary setting for both King's and Kubrick's versions of *The Shining*: the Overlook Hotel.

Acknowledgments

Thank you to the editors of the following publications in which many of these poems first appeared.

Dissonance Magazine: "Preachers of Impermanence," "Living Will," "Session One"
Into the Void: "What the Beast Desires"
Unvael: "Morbid Curiosity"
Humana Obscura: "Indigo"
VAINE Magazine: "Transmission of Dead Air," "Contagion"
Drunk Monkeys: "Savior Complex"
The Closed Eye Open: "Suffering"

Thank you to *Red Noise Collective* as well for publishing the collage "Confidence" in their beautiful journal.

I would also like to sincerely thank the following people that helped build me up to make this book possible:

Dave Edwards, Katelyn Edwards, and Kevin Pelc, thank you for seeking out help for me when I needed it most. I cannot properly express how much that meant to me, but I will be forever grateful for your kindness and understanding.

Jon Page and Wesley Rice, thank you for not only being the biggest supporters of any creative endeavor I set my sights on, but also for your insights and friendship. You're both a powerful support system, and I appreciate that beyond words.

Jared Downing and Tylor Olson, thank you for your understanding during the worst period of my life and your willingness to push me beyond what I ever thought I was capable of. You are both like brothers to me, and I am sincerely grateful to have you in my life.

Thank you to my mother and stepfather, Danie and Ed Maynes; my sisters, Allie and Parker Maynes; and my grandmother, Sharon Handville. Your love and continued support of my creative endeavors has always meant the world to me. It continues to be a source of lifeblood whenever I feel particularly inanimate, and I appreciate your continued efforts towards vitalizing my life and my work.

Thank you to Valerie Valentine for your valuable insights and suggestions during the editing process. I appreciate you taking this journey with me and utilizing your skills to help shape my work into its best possible form. Without your help, this book would not be the same.

Amanda Allen, whatever invisible shackles I seem to imprison myself in, whether through spiraling thoughts, creative stagnation, or disheartening self-condemnation, you provide a key for through your unconditional love and support, through your patience and understanding, through your thought-provoking reframing and the hope you provide. You consistently help me break free from my cranium cage, and I see the completion of this book as my most daring escape yet. Finishing this project would not have been possible without your presence in my life. Thank you for your help in making the hope scattered throughout this book, the hope I feel now, genuine.

To anyone that has supported my previous books, *Internalize* and *Drowning in the Ink of Oblivion*, thank you. Readers will always be the ones perpetuating the pulse of a writer's work, and without you, my words would have died long ago. You have given me an opportunity to be with you on the page, and I'm honored to share that with you. Thank you for returning, and I hope you enjoyed this book.

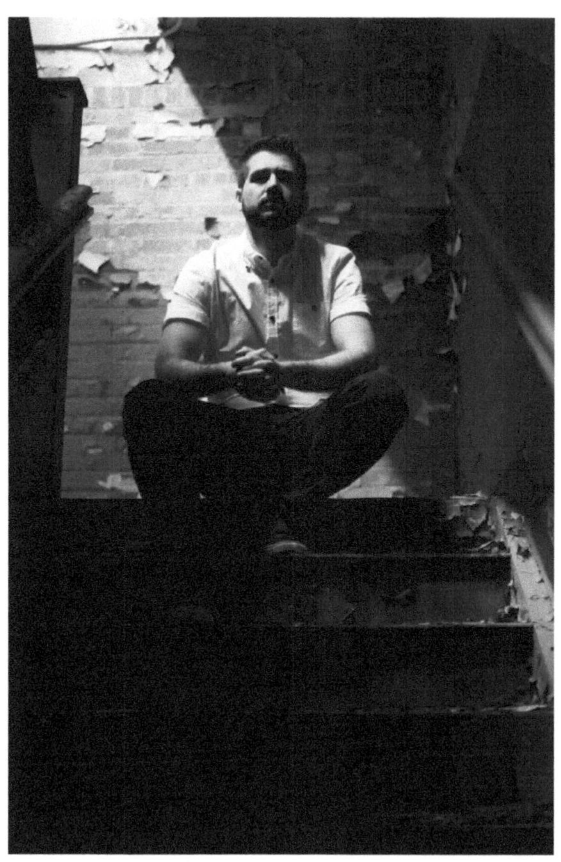

Author Photo: Tylor Olson

J.A. HANDVILLE is a poet and visual artist based in Syracuse, New York, and the author of *Internalize* (2018) and *Drowning in the Ink of Oblivion* (2021). In between consuming copious amounts of coffee, J.A. Handville creates collages and poetry often themed around the difficulties of love, mental illness, and the human condition. J.A. Handville's work has been published in *Unvael, Into the Void, Dissonance Magazine, VAINE Magazine, Humana Obscura, Drunk Monkeys, The Closed Eye Open,* and *Red Noise Collective.*

www.ingramcontent.com/pod-product-compliance
Lightning Source LLC
LaVergne TN
LVHW052255100826
845147LV00001B/56

9798992748000